The
Music
Geek's
Bible

The Music Geek's Bible

Mike Evans

MQP

MQ Publications Ltd

Published by MQ Publications Limited
12 The Ivories
6-8 Northampton Street
London, N1 2HY
Tel: +44 (0)20 7359 2244
Fax: +44 (0)20 7359 1616
E-mail: mail@mqpublications.com
Web site: www.mqpublications.com

North American office
49 West 24th Street
New York, NY 10010
E-mail: information@mqpublicationsus.com

Contributors: Simon Hankin and Warwick Worldwide

ISBN: 1-84072-799-3

9 8 7 6 5 4 3 2 1

Printed in China

The publisher does not endorse the illegal downloading of any
music. Furthermore, readers should be aware that music
products and Web sites listed in this work may have changed or
disappeared between when this work was written and when it is
read. At the time of publication, all songs and albums are
available for legal downloading.

CONTENTS

INTRODUCTION

Music, in all its rich diversity, makes up the soundtrack of our lives. It can be great art, wonderful entertainment, something to dance to, an affirmation of a particular attitude or lifestyle, or just a seemingly trivial diversion. It unites, divides, and defines us, and we all have something to say about it. In celebrating some of the most groundbreaking, astounding, memorable, uplifting, expertly crafted, or just plain enjoyable pieces of popular music ever made, I am hoping to give you even more to say about it.

New technology has created a digital music revolution in recent years, which has generated even more controversy and debate, and looks set to change the face of the recording industry forever. Thanks to the Internet and modern digital technology, an immense variety of music is available as never before, and this book aims to get *you* in on the downloading act. It's actually much easier than you might think! As well as being a complete user's guide to all the basics about legally downloading music, creating a digital music library, and listening to it on the latest and most stylish MP3 player, this book is a guide to the greatest sounds now available to you at the push of a button—or the click of a mouse!

Simply by surfing the Web, you can quickly and easily discover an array of new musical gems and rediscover old classics—with the added bonus that, if you only like one song by a particular band, you can buy it as a single track instead of wasting money on a whole album. The Internet is like a jukebox, but with an almost infinite number of choices, and, with this book, I'm giving you a place to start. These are some of the most crucial, must-have tracks available online *right now*.

You'll find no order of preference here, so there should be no arguments about who's best and who comes before whom, but, inevitably, there will be disagreements about my final choices. Perhaps there are some omissions you will find conspicuous, or inclusions you think ludicrous—I remember one or two songs that qualified for inclusion by virtue of their being so unforgettably awful! Occasionally, I've also recommended a complete album (indicated in italics) as worthy of downloading in its entirety.

At the end of the day, it's all down to individual judgment and taste—"or lack of," I hear someone say—but I hope I've covered most of the classic pieces, leading artists, and major styles. I make no apologies for crucial names, such as Elvis Presley and Bob Dylan, appearing more than once; their wealth of output simply can't be reflected in one single song.

Certain pieces that I would love to include had to be omitted because they simply aren't available at the moment. Some artists have yet to allow their music to be available for legal downloading—The Beatles being the most famous case in point—but it's a situation that's changing all the time. Crucially, every song included here has been checked to ensure its availability on legal online music stores—I cannot stress too strongly the importance of only downloading *legally* available material.

The big record labels are adding more music to their digital catalogs every day. So, by the time you read this, some of the tracks we couldn't include will probably be available, including—with any luck—music by The Beatles and the other remaining holdouts. Likewise, computer and digital music technology is changing all the time. No doubt, within months of my writing this, there will be dozens of new online stores offering new and improved ways to download music, not to mention countless smaller, more advanced, and sexier-looking MP3 players.

Think of this book as a giant jukebox on the printed page. You can dip into it wherever you please, and as often as you like, before you make your music selection in cyberspace. Hopefully, the hundreds of tracks and albums included here will convey at least a hint of the sheer *richness* of popular music—which is now more accessible than at any time in its long and varied history.

Mike Evans, September 2005

all about downloading

a BRIEF HISTORY

Once upon a time, well back in 1999 to be precise, Shawn Fanning–the godfather of downloading–started a music revolution when he came up with "Napster," a music-sharing service that provided illegal downloads to millions of people worldwide. Unsurprisingly, it was a massive success–not bad for a teenage college student, huh?

The deal was that Napster allowed individual surfers to upload their own music collections onto a central server and share them–for free–with one another. A great idea? Eighty million registered users thought so. But heavy metal band Metallica and the Recording Industry Association of America (RIAA) had other ideas. The RIAA tried to shut down Napster after just six months and Metallica tried to sue the individual users because the musicians, songwriters, producers, and record companies obviously weren't making any cash out of these free downloads.

After Napster came "KaZaA," which proved an even bigger headache for royalty-hungry record labels. KaZaA used a different sharing system that meant every KaZaA user became their own server while they were online, so there was no central operation to shut down. Though this kept KaZaA out of the law courts, a few users weren't so lucky: frustrated, the RIAA began suing individual "music pirates" for thousands of dollars!

The battle raged on until 2003, when Apple wrested back control by launching its own *legal* downloading program. Named "iTunes," the service allows users to download individual tracks for 99¢ each. A new legalized version of Napster swiftly followed, along with "My Coke Music" and numerous other programs, each offering their own unique selling points for download junkies–and all with the added attraction that they wouldn't get you busted!

The record labels had finally decided if you can't beat 'em, join 'em–and the gamble certainly paid off! In 2004, music downloads generated $330 million, and with that figure set to rise dramatically in 2005, downloading is now a huge player in the future of music.

WHAT YOU NEED

Now that you've decided you're ready to jump on the bandwagon and get into downloading, you've got to have the right stuff. So here's our guide to all the technical bits and pieces your computer needs (we're kinda assuming you already have the basics, like a modem, monitor, keyboard...) if you want to start buying, downloading, and boogying along to the latest and greatest music hits on the Web.

System Requirements

Some of this may look a little techie and complicated, but read on because these are the minimum system requirements your computer has to have before you can start downloading and listening to music. If your computer has been hanging around for a while, I'm afraid you may need to look into an upgrade:

Windows PC
Windows XP or 2000
500 MHz Pentium class processor or better
128 MB RAM minimum/256 MB RAM recommended
Latest Windows service packs recommended, including a
supported CD-RW drive to burn CDs, a video display card,
and a QuickTime 6.5 soundcard.

Mac
Mac OS X v10.1.5 or later
400MHz G3 processor or better
128 MB RAM minimum/256 MB RAM recommended
QuickTime 6.2 required to encode AAC files.

PCs vs. Macs

You can download music on both PCs and Macs (hurrah!), but only certain download programs will work with certain computers (boo!).

The bottom line is this: it doesn't much matter whether you plump for a Mac or a PC, just so long as you recognize that each is compatible with different file types and different download services, which means you have to make a commitment to one or the other from the beginning. Otherwise, if you want to transfer your tracks from a PC to a Mac or vice versa, or connect your digital music player to one type of computer and then the other, you're likely to stumble across any number of problems, as outlined throughout this chapter. It's also worth noting that some people think Macs suffer far less from virus threats than their PC counterparts. Me? I'm on the fence.

Get to know which file types your chosen computer and player can support, so you don't end up wasting time trying to download incompatible tracks. Here's a quick guide to the main file formats, or "codecs" as they're known:

MP3 (Short for MPEG-1, Audio Layer 3)

When music downloading was still a wee baby, the MP3 was by far the most popular codec around. And it has remained popular because it's simply so versatile. A real all-rounder, an MP3 file will operate on every brand of digital music player as well as on other digital products.

AAC (Short for MPEG-4 AAC)

The AAC (short for Advanced Audio Coding, fact fans) is like an MP3, but with just that little bit more. It offers a higher-quality sound than the MP3 and needs less data to get the same job done, giving better audio results. For this reason, the Apple iTunes Music Store sells all its tracks in the AAC format. Sounds great? But hold up, there's a catch—AAC Protected files can *only* be played on your computer through iTunes or on an iPod, which is bad news if you've bought a different brand of player.

If you import songs from a music CD using the AAC format, you can still convert them into more versatile MP3 files, which you can then transfer onto *any* digital music player you like. But this isn't the case with any tracks you buy and download from iTunes, because they arrive in a special AAC Protected format.

To transfer music that you've downloaded from iTunes to another device, you will first need to burn the track onto a blank CD, *then* import it onto your chosen Windows PC music program, and *finally* copy the track onto your music player. Phew!

WMA (Short for Windows Media Audio)

These files are compatible with pretty much every download program (with the exception of iTunes). But if you're using an older Mac, you may not be able to support WMAs. The deal with a WMA is that it offers the same sound quality as an MP3 file, but at only half the file size.

WAV

This file type is a joint effort between Microsoft and IBM, and it can—for the time being at least—lay claim to being the highest quality audio format available on any computer. So there!

USB or FireWire?

At the risk of sounding all techie here, we're talking cables. USB and FireWire are different types of cable, both of which hook up your digital music player to your computer, so you can transfer music files from one to the other.

You'll probably find that you won't have to choose between one type of cable or the other, because most players are sold with them as standard. But just so you know, USB is the most popular choice of cable because it works with both Macs and PCs. FireWire, on the other hand, is faster, but it mainly only does the business with Macs.

Broadband

Surfing the Internet can be about as much fun as watching paint dry with an average dial-up connection, but broadband offers you the chance to transfer files from the Web at superfast speed. That really is fantastic news for all you wannabe-downloaders because broadband makes it dead easy and super speedy to download all of your favorite music tracks.

Shop around before choosing your broadband provider because there are so many different deals out there. And be sure to check out all the terms of your agreement carefully *before* you sign up, as some companies impose a limit on the amount of megabytes you can download each month. Go over that limit and you'll be charged for it—and it won't be cheap!

If you're not already hooked up, you can check out who's providing broadband in your area on these Web sites:

- www.Broadband.com
- www.Broadbandbuyer.com
- www.Broadbandreports.com
- www.Getconnected.com

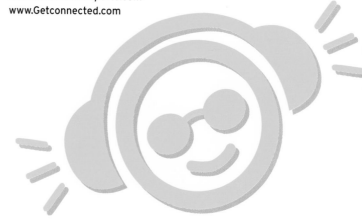

DiGiTaL MuSiC PLaYeRS

In a market that is now positively *heaving* with digital music players—aka MP3 players—it can be tricky to know which model to go for. And yes, the choice is more complicated than which one has the cutest little buttons!

Take memory for example: there are now three types of memory drive available for MP3 players. They are:

- Hard drive
- Micro drive
- Flash drive

What's the difference? Well, most digital music players these days store all their information on a hard drive, just like computers. But players that use flash cards are becoming more popular because they sidestep the irritating "skipping" sometimes associated with hard drives. Flash players are smaller than their hard drive-based cousins, but can't carry nearly as many songs. As for micro drive players, these operate along the same lines as the hard drives, but are more compact and have a slightly lower storage capacity.

As a general rule of thumb, if you plan to use your player in a very active way—down the gym or jogging—you're probably better off investing in a flash-based product. But if you just want to store all your music in one place—and it's only your ears you want to exercise—a hard drive may be more your thing.

Here's our guide to the biggest hitters available in stores right now. It's just a taster of the many delights on offer in a market flooded with swish digital music players. Other brands to check out include Dell, Philips, Toshiba, Samsung, and Sony. But before you buy anything, remember that some of the big brands won't work with Macs. It's also a great idea to ask your friends what they think of their players and to check out the Internet and trade magazines for reviews on all the latest gizmos and gadgets. Happy shopping!

iPod

The daddy of MP3 players, the iPod has quickly burrowed its way into the hearts and minds of millions. Already a design classic, the iPod features a 2-inch monochrome backlit screen on its trademark white body, with matching ear buds.

It has a standard storage size of 20GB, allowing you to store up to 5,000 tracks—the new 60GB color screen model stores 15,000—and you can rifle through your songs, albums, and extra functions (calendar, games etc) via a handy touch-sensitive "click wheel." The iPod also has a handy playlist function, so you can organize your songs by mood, genre, or whatever you fancy, and "Shuffle Songs" plays your tunes in random order. All this and it weighs just 5.6 ounces and boasts 12 hours of rechargeable battery life.

Apple's micro drive model is the colorful iPod Mini, which is proving even more popular than its big brother. Weighing just 3.6 ounces and available with either 4 or 6GB of storage, it is cheaper and smaller than the original. The iPod Shuffle is the brand's flash-based baby—it holds far fewer songs, but is much smaller and great for active types who are always on the go.

Just released onto the market is the newest in the Russian-doll-like range of iPod players—the iPod Nano. It comes with 2 or 4GB of storage and plays for up to 14 hours between charges. It also has a color screen, which displays the album art for the song you're listening to, and you can also use it to store and view photos. Simply put, the Nano is 100 percent iPod—but it weighs just 1.5 ounces and is as thin as a pencil!

Creative

Creative music players are known for their hardiness and their long battery life—in fact, the Zen Touch boasts a massive 24 hours of continuous play, double that of the iPod. At 20 or 40GB, this glossy white player has a similar storage size to the iPod, though it's a fair bit heavier, weighing in at 7.1 ounces. It's also well regarded for its impressive sound quality and the fact that it's so simple to use. The Touch Pad allows for easy navigation, you can name your playlists, and you have the option of listening to FM radio on it too.

The Creative Zen Micro is—you guessed it—one of the line's micro drive options and it is available with either 4, 5, or 6GB of storage, while the MuVo TX is a flash alternative.

iRiver

The sleek iRiver U10 (available in 2GB, 1GB, and 512MB) has plenty going for it. It features a large, high-resolution display that dispenses with buttons and integrates them on the screen borders. As well as photo and video viewing, FM radio tuning, and recording capabilities, this compact little player can be accessorized with a futuristic docking station and convenient infrared remote control.

Check out the iRiver H10 range for vibrant, color-screen players with memory sizes ranging from 5 to 20GB.

DOWNLOADING MUSIC: A USER'S GUIDE

Ok, you've bought the newest, trendiest player and got all the latest stuff for your computer, so now you need the knowledge. Here's all you need to know to get downloading with the best of 'em:

Download Programs and Online Music Stores

iTunes, Napster, Rhapsody...the Internet is becoming increasingly jampacked with legal places to buy your favorite tunes, each offering their customers slightly different deals. In general, all the sites offer the same thing in terms of the music. The different services have done deals with the same big record labels and, as EMI, BMG, Sony, and the rest deliver all their digitized catalog in one go, it's fair to say that if a track is available on iTunes, it's probably available on most of the other services, too.

Where they tend to differ is in terms of payment and license agreements (stuff like how often you can burn a downloaded track onto CD), which vary from site to site. We know it's a bore, but it's really worth reading the small print to find out all the nitty gritties.

For a detailed list of all the legal download sites available on the net, log on to www.pro-music.org or www.whatsthedownload.com, but here's the lowdown on the biggest programs out there right now:

iTunes
http://www.apple.com/itunes
The original legal download service and still one of the best. iTunes announced in July 2005 that its users had downloaded a massive

half a billion songs in the two years it's been in business, so these guys must be doing something right, right?

The site claims to have the largest downloadable library out there with a monster 1.5 million songs available for you to peruse at leisure, including some out-of-print classics and exclusive tracks from the world's biggest acts. It's pretty easy to find your way around the site, although some of the explanations are a bit long-winded. You can even check out their video library and ever-growing podcast (page 31) directory free-of charge.

iTunes charges a flat fee of 99¢ (79p) for each downloaded track and $9.95 (£7.99) for each album, payable by credit card or the online payment system PayPal. U.K. iTunes customers currently pay 20 percent more for downloads than their French and German counterparts, but the European commission is investigating, so it could all change!

Napster
http://www.napster.com

Napster Mark 2 (aka the legal version) is a slick operation. With a back catalog of more than a million tracks, the Napster site also allows you to listen to a whole host of radio stations. And the budding DJs among you can even create your own radio station based around your most cutting-edge playlists. If that's not enough, they've got 45-years-worth of the charts online, which makes finding anything from your aunt's favorite Sinatra ballad to the corny song you all danced to back in high school, a breeze.

To really get to grips with everything the site has to offer, check out its handy tutorial. It explains how to make the most of Napster's features in a way that's dead simple to understand.

Napster offers two ways to get your hands on its goodies. The first is like the iTunes system—you can buy and download individual songs for a set fee, starting at 80¢ (68p) each. Alternatively, you can subscribe to Napster for $9.95 (£9.95) per month. This gives you unlimited access, allowing you to download as many tracks as you like—but you're only "renting" these downloads, if you cancel your subscription, you won't be able to listen to them anymore.

Rhapsody

http://www.rhapsody.com

Rhapsody is another big American player in the download wars that works on similar lines to Napster and iTunes. You have to become a member before you can make use of both its download and its radio services. But they do offer a free trial, so you can try before you buy and make sure you're happy with the system before deciding to part with your hard-earned cash.

If you do sign up, you'll find more than a million tunes at your fingertips. Rhapsody's music download services are only available in the U.S. right now, but this looks set to change in the future. And, if you live elsewhere, you can still use the site's jukebox software in the meantime.

My Coke Music

http://www.mycokemusic.com

My Coke Music is a straightforward site with a straightforward function from the massive conglomerate. They've also been offering the chance to win free downloads on cans of their famous soft drinks.

Surf your way onto this Web page and you can simply buy and download tracks, without any of those extra trimmings that some of its competitors offer. There are a few great added features though, including the chart listings and featured artist sections, as well as themed playlists, like "Closet Classics" and "Movie Madness," which encourage you to discover new musical gems and rediscover those old forgotten favorites.

For the time being, My Coke Music is only available in the U.K. and parts of Europe, and 80p will get you a single download or 99 one-off "streams." For more detailed info on how to use the site, plus the lowdown on exactly what it's got going on online, head straight for the site's useful Help section.

eMusic

http://www.emusic.com

If all these mainstream offerings leave you cold, why not check out indie specialists eMusic. Featuring tracks from the smaller, obscure labels as well as the majors, eMusic boasts a library of some 600,000 tracks, from emerging as well as established artists, in all music styles from punk, electronica, and reggae to country.

While you have to sign up to this site as well, it does offer a two-week trial period during which you can download tracks to keep forever, whether or not you decide to subscribe at the end—it's got to be worth a look.

Big Noise Music
http://www.bignoisemusic.com

Launched as part of Oxfam's "Make Trade Fair" charity campaign, this is the site for music lovers with social consciences as deep as their pockets. Tracks are a snip, starting at just 75p, and with 10 percent of everything spent on the site going to the charity, you know that some of your money is going to a good cause. There are currently 750,000 tracks on offer from 30,000 artists, but right now the site is only available to PC users within Europe.

MP3 Unsigned
http://www.mp3unsigned.com

If you want to make sure you're always at the cutting edge of all things musical, take a look around MP3 Unsigned. This site simply provides a showcase for unsigned acts, taking in every imaginable genre along the way. Including artist biographies and full-length track previews, MP3 Unsigned is a great introduction to what's new in music—straightforward to use and appealingly rough around the edges.

eClassical
http://www.eclassical.com

Although you can download classical music from the big players already mentioned, these guys are the specialists. The world's biggest classical music shop is easy to use, offers single tracks from only 49¢, as well as free daily downloads, and even allows you to search by mood—there really are good tunes to listen to when you're hungover, feeling romantic, ironing, or when life just sucks!

Free Legal Downloading

For the most part, if a download is legal you're going to have to pay for it—podcasting being the obvious exception, but more of that later (page 31). However, there are still a few legal ways to download music for free, especially if you're looking for work from new artists and independent labels.

First up, why not try your favorite band or singer's official Web site? These sometimes offer free downloads and exclusive online mixes for fans, plus community chat areas where you can discuss just what you think of their music with other enthusiasts.

One of the best sites to check out is Internet giant Amazon, which offers free legal MP3 downloads across a range of genres. As with other Amazon products, you can read users' comments on their site and leave your own reviews of their downloadable tracks. You can also upload MP3s you've created yourself via Amazon's Digital Music Network.

Other sites worth taking a look at include:

http://www.soundclick.com

http://www.ampcast.com

http://www.iuma.com

http://www.vitaminic.com

http://www.epitonic.com

http://www.archive.org/audio/netlabels.php

http://www.archive.org/audio/etreelisting-browse.php

http://www.purevolume.com

http://www.ic-musicmedia.com

http://www.theweedfiles.com

http://www.freechildrensmusic.com

Downloading Singles and Albums

Downloading from any of the legal Web sites I've just mentioned should be a simple, safe, and hassle-free experience. All of the main sites, like iTunes and Napster, come complete with their own step-by-step instructions for downloading music, as well as advice on system requirements and compatibility issues etc, but here's a quick guide to getting started:

Finding What You Want:

1. On your first visit to any site, follow their instructions to download the relevant software onto your computer. This will give you access to all the tracks available for purchase.

2. You can then search by artist, album, song, or genre, or use the site's special search tools to track down songs in the charts, playing on the radio, or recommended by celebrities.

3. Once you've found what you're after, simply click on the artist's name, album artwork, or song title to read a full biography and reviews, as well as find out about the other tracks available.

4. Next, click to hear a 30-second preview of your chosen song—just to make sure you're buying what you think you are!

Downloading Music:

1. Once you're sure you've found the song you want, simply click on the "Buy Track" box and follow the instructions to pay for and download your chosen track. At this point, you'll need to sign into the service if you haven't done so already.

2. You can keep an eye on how long the download will take by looking at the "Download Status" button at the top of the page.

3. Your music is then stored in your own "Library" on your chosen music store, and from there you can organize it into playlists.

4. It is also automatically stored on your own computer (in your digital music library), from where you can burn it to CD, add it to a playlist, sync it with your music player, or just listen to it!

5. You can also organize and label the tracks in your library, via MP3 tagging, to create playlists and sub-divisions. Don't worry, it's not complicated—all will be revealed below.

Creating Playlists Online

Download programs do more than just sell music, you know. They allow you to organize all your tunes into as many playlists as you like, making it easy for you to look like a bona fide MP3 DJ in next to no time! Here's a start-up guide to making playlists work for you:

The Playlist

You can create playlists according to genre, mood, or activity, or even based on the tunes you listen to most often, or the songs of a specific genre you've added to your library within the past week. Basically, you can be as freakishly organized as you like!

Once you've decided what sort of mood you're in and what kind of playlist you want, all you have to do is type in your command and the online software will get the job done for you. From there you can create "Smart Playlists," which subdivide the tracks even further—so you can guarantee you'll have the perfect playlists to cater for every whim, mood, and scenario.

Get the Party Started

Need a party playlist but don't have the time to create one? Don't worry, you can use "Party Shuffle" to make sure you get the right tunes at the click of a button. The Party Shuffle service basically picks out a random selection of tracks either from your entire online library, or from a selected playlist.

If a particularly dodgy or embarrassing number suddenly rears its ugly head, no worries! You can also delete upcoming songs from the list before they're played—and keep your street cred in front of your mates. And hey, if the shuffled-up party mix worked for you, you can always save it to use as a playlist at your next party.

Share Your Playlists

Most download stores offer a great service where by you can share your playlists with your mates. So if you're feeling generous, you can let the people in your life browse—and rate!—any of your playlists on your chosen store. Check out the various sites for more details.

Rate and Track Your Music

Be the music buff you've always wanted to be and assign star ratings to any of the tracks in your library. And if you want to know how obsessed you've become with a particular track, you can also check out how many times you've played it with "Play Count" and when you last gave it a spin with the "Last Played" facility.

Printing Playlists

A lot of download stores allow you to print hard copies of any of your playlists, or even your entire library. So you'll never lose track of what albums or singles you've got, or be able to lie about not downloading that embarrassing, novelty Christmas song last year!

Burning Music to CD

If you want to listen to your music in your car or anywhere other than on your computer, here's how to transfer your playlists to CD:

1. Insert a blank CD-R disc into your computer's CD-R burner.

2. Click the "Burn" or "Rip" button on your playlist window, and follow the instructions to specify what you want to download.

3. Before you finally burn your playlist to CD, don't forget to double-check how many times your download program allows you to do so: they often set a limit of five times per playlist.

Burning Music from CD

As well as downloading new tunes from the stores on the Web, you've probably also got a stack of CDs you want to listen to on your computer or transfer to your shiny new MP3 player. This is known as "ripping," and it's really rather easy:

1. Shut down all other applications on your computer, but make sure you're online.

2. Put your chosen CD into the CD drive and, if your music software program doesn't open automatically, open it yourself, and wait for it to identify your CD.

3. Select which tracks you want to import onto your computer, click the button, and go!

4. Your tracks will appear in your library within minutes. Then you can either just play them on your computer, organize them into playlists, or download them onto your music player.

Transferring to Your MP3 Player

Here's how to get your freshly downloaded tracks onto your digital music player so you can listen to them on the go:

1. As always, close all the applications on your computer.

2. Open your music playing software, and click the "Burn" button.

3. Hook your MP3 player up to the computer. If it's your first time downloading onto this player, you'll need to look under "Tasks" for the "Add a New Device" option. Select your product for installation and follow the simple onscreen instructions.

4. Choose your tracks and click "Add to Selected Device."

5. Finally, click "Start Transfer" and watch that music fly!

DOWNLOADING TIPS

To get the best out of your downloading experience and make it as simple and speedy as possible, both your computer and Internet connection need to be performing at their best. If they're being a bit awkward and sluggish, here are a few tips to help you figure out what's ailing them:

1. The first thing to try in this scenario is the "power-cycle." Basically, unplug your Internet cable for a few seconds, and then reconnect to a—hopefully—faster service.

2. That hasn't done the trick? Most broadband Internet Service Providers (ISPs) offer a download rate ranging from 256 kilobits per second to 1.5 megabits per second. But you might not always be getting what you're paying for.

    It might sound complicated, but it's actually quite easy to check. You simply need to time how long it takes for your computer to download, say, a 5 megabit file from your ISP. Once the file is downloaded, click on the file to get its Properties. You can then divide the file's size in bytes by the time in seconds that it took to download it. Then, multiply that by ten and you've got your megabit download speed.

    If you do this a few times and record the average you can find out what your download rate really is. If you find you're getting a rate much slower than what you're paying for, get onto your ISP right away—you don't want to wait any longer for that latest chart-topping pop single than you have to!

3. Finally, to keep things running smoothly, look into installing some sort of firewall and router software to protect your computer and all your new kit and music downloads from virus and scanning threats.

Avoiding Viruses

Getting a computer virus can be just like catching a bad cold. First you get the snuffles, then you ache all over, until finally you're completely laid up. So it is with your computer; it starts with just a minor glitch here or there, then the virus wreaks total havoc with your machine—and none of us are safe. Downloading loads of files from the Internet only makes things riskier.

To see the damage a virus can do, take a look at the "Love Bug." This romantically-named little critter ran amok in 2005, attacking a staggering 55 million computers and causing more than $8.7 billion worth of damage. With up to 12 new viruses cropping up every day, this was far from a freak incident, so it's really important to keep your computer all safe and protected.

Here are a few simple tips for safer downloading that just might help you avoid the next big bug:

1. Invest in some anti-virus software. Once installed, the program will automatically check for viruses every time you insert a new CD-Rom or surf the Net. Make sure you regularly run an "Auto Update" (once a week is recommended) to keep your virus protection right up to date.

2. Other ways of keeping your computer virus-free include: not opening e-mail attachments from unknown sources, disabling macros in your applications, and using Windows XP (if you have it) to automatically update your software patches and virus-busting software.

3. Finally, along with spam e-mails, downloading any kind of files or programs from illegal or untrustworthy sites is one of the biggest culprits when it comes to infecting your computer with irksome viruses. So, play it safe, and stick to the legal sites.

Legal Issues

Who Controls Downloading?

Two main organizations keep their beady eyes on music download activity: the RIAA (Recording Industry Association of America) and the BPI (British Phonographic Industry). They represent the interests of the record companies, so they definitely won't be on your side if you're illegally downloading and sharing music files.

What Is Illegal?

Well, pretty much everything that's free. That's because all songs are protected by copyright law, which means that the clever musicians, songwriters, producers, and everyone else involved in creating them can control what happens to their musical babies—and get the financial rewards for all their hard work. Put simply, if you're sneaking in a bit of non-authorized downloading, the chances are you're breaking the law.

Peer-to-peer file-sharing (that's sharing files with your mates and other people online, to you and me) is the most common form of illegal downloading these days. So yes, even just giving your fave band's latest track to a friend could land you in hot water!

Digital Rights Management

DRM is the system that controls copying, downloading, and sharing music. Make sure you take a look at the DRM restrictions on any track you're downloading or any new CDs you buy because some have strict rules about exactly how you can use them and how many times you can copy them. It's best to check this stuff out at the start, rather than just assuming you're safe because you're surfing a legal site—and it'll help you avoid disappointments later.

What Are the Penalties?

If you're downloading illegally, getting busted could seriously cramp your financial style! Forget all that stuff you've heard about music-types just doing it for their art; the record industry is a hard-nosed, squillion-dollar business. And when something threatens their success, the record labels get serious. With CD sales worldwide plummeting 20 percent since 1999, they're not messing around when it comes to illegal downloaders.

Both the RIAA and BPI proved they can play hardball when they began prosecuting individual downloaders, who thought they were safe sitting at home in front of their computers. The RIAA even pursued a case against a 12-year-old girl who'd been caught downloading nursery rhymes! If you're found guilty, the bill can run into the thousands.

The basic rule of thumb when it comes to downloading music is: If you're paying for it, it's probably legal; if you're not, then it's probably not. So, make sure you know exactly what you're getting into before you start. And remember, although it's legal to burn your CDs to MP3 for your own personal use, it's illegal to upload them onto the Web so anyone else can access or download them.

Before you start railing against the system, think of it this way: None of us expected music to be free before the Internet introduced us to the brave new world of downloading. Even a three-minute music clip represents months of work for scores of musicians, singers, and producers, so putting your hand in your pocket to pay for their efforts is really only fair. It's not just record company bosses in sharp suits who feel the pinch from illegal downloads—missing out on royalties can hit the "little people" hard, especially the up-and-coming acts, the session musicians, and the small, independent labels, who often have to do double the work.

So cough up! And as well as basking in the warm glow of doing the right thing and supporting new music, rest assured that your shiny new track is probably better quality than any illegal version and less likely to give your computer some virus-related pox. Hurrah!

PODCASTING AND THE FUTURE

Currently being touted as the future of digital music, "podcasting" is already here and doing increasingly big business. But what exactly is it?

The best way to explain podcasting is to look at its name, which is a blend of "iPod" and "broadcasting." From that, the techno whizzkids among you can probably figure out that podcasting is a kind of digital broadcasting. It allows you to upload audio files via the Internet onto your own "feed," other people can then subscribe to that feed and automatically receive new files from it. Basically, it's kind of like having your own radio show.

Broadcasting giants Clear Channel Radio, Infinity, and the BBC have all recently set up "feeds" for several of their radio shows—and many other radio stations, big and small, are set to follow in their footsteps. Podcast users can sign up to receive each and every episode of their chosen show directly onto their computer—for free!

The beauty of these podcast files is they don't have to stay on your computer, you can sync them onto any MP3 player with audio-playing software and listen to them on the go. Members of the iPod posse will even find that a podcast option appears on their menu as soon as they sign up to a feed.

Understandably, everyone from amateur DJs to commercial radio stations, religious groups to schools—not to mention people wishing to bypass the censors—has begun jumping on the podcast bandwagon. So now it's not just your music you can take with you on the move; it's your whole lifestyle.

With Apple recently adding a podcast directory to the iTunes music store—and reporting a staggering one million subscriptions in just two days—and video podcasting just around the corner, it's clear that this is the true future of downloading.

PURE POP

The British painter Richard Hamilton once described all things pop as "popular, transient, expendable, low cost, mass-produced, young, witty, gimmicky, glamorous, and big business." Certainly much of this—forgetting "low cost" in most cases—applies to what we might call pure pop: music with the prime function of making money by having as wide an appeal as possible. However, within those parameters many undisputed pop classics have emerged, despite often originally having a perceived shelf life of a few months at the most. Expertly crafted, to the point, perfectly of their time, and highly memorable (sometimes annoyingly so!)— these are all definitions we could add to describe some of the best examples of pure pop.

Hound Dog / Don't Be Cruel
Elvis Presley | 1956

The most popular double hit single in music history: both sides reached the Number One spot on the U.S. Billboard chart, alternating in the pole position for a grand total of 11 weeks! A raw blues-driven rocker backed with a country-tinged masterpiece, both were completely of their time and unrepeatable. This was Elvis Presley at his peak.

Karma Chameleon
Culture Club | 1983

Boy George and group stormed the charts, reaching Number One in both the U.S. and the U.K., with this song's catchy sing-along chorus: "Red, gold, and green..."

Some Kind of a Summer
David Cassidy | 1973

Wispy-voiced Cassidy was a teenybopper sensation in the early '70s, and this gentle evocation of hot days and balmy evenings has managed—perhaps surprisingly—to stand the test of time.

Wannabe
The Spice Girls | 1996

Girl-power popsters supreme, Baby, Posh, Scary, Ginger, and Sporty Spice were simply the biggest thing in the mid '90s. This debut single, which hit the top of the charts in a massive 31 countries, said it all—"I'll tell you what I want, what I really really want."

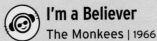

I'm a Believer
The Monkees | 1966

With a song penned by Neil Diamond, the "manufactured" Monkees sound pretty genuine here. Regardless of the controversy over who was really playing and singing on the track, this is a pop classic.

ABC
Jackson 5 | 1970

Despite strong competition from fellow family pop act, the Osmonds, the high-energy Jackson 5 were the teenybop sensations of the early '70s. In this, their best-known hit, they tried to teach us "how easy love can be."

Wonderwall
Oasis | 1995

Britpop band Oasis—and more specifically the band's songwriter Noel Gallagher—show their most lyrical side in this melodic mini-masterpiece.

Rock Your Body
Justin Timberlake | 2002

The marriage of the year's must-have producers, the Neptunes, (famed for work with Ol' Dirty Bastard, No Doubt, Kelis, and Britney Spears) with *NSYNC's newly-shorn gonnabe star Justin Timberlake delivered on every level. "Rock Your Body" was the most dance-orientated track from his Grammy Award-winning album *Justified*, which sold three million copies in the U.S. and more than seven million worldwide.

Take a Chance on Me
Abba | 1978

Love it or loathe it, Abba's slickly synchronized brand of pop left us with a mountain of catchy melodies that you just can't get out of your head–even though in many cases you might want to! An essential part of the sound of the '70s.

You've Lost That Lovin' Feelin'
The Righteous Brothers | 1964

This was one of the greatest pop productions of all time and a landmark in the creative development of record producer Phil Spector. As a piece of studio artistry, "You've Lost That Lovin' Feelin'" was rarely equaled and its simple opening line resonates just as effectively today, "You never close your eyes anymore..."

River Deep, Mountain High
Ike and Tina Turner | 1966

Although this only got to Number 88 in the U.S. charts, it was one of Phil Spector's epic productions and a storming hit by vocalist Tina. Simply awesome.

(What a) Wonderful World
Sam Cooke | 1959

Not to be confused with the entirely different Louis Armstrong hit with the same name, this song is sometimes better known by its first line, "Don't know much about history..." The lilting voice of Sam Cooke celebrates love as enough to make the world a wonderful place–something you just can't get from books.

I Should Be So Lucky
Kylie Minogue | 1988

Another example of happy-pop that sticks with you even when you wish it would go away! Kylie's popular role in an Australian soap opera was followed by this archetypal piece of dance froth by slick '80s songwriters and producers Stock, Aitken, and Waterman.

Kung Fu Fighting
Carl Douglas | 1974

Cashing in on the kung-fu craze triggered by the popular Bruce Lee martial arts movies of the early '70s, this sole hit for Jamaican-born R&B singer Douglas reached the top of both the U.S. and U.K. music charts.

Fever
Peggy Lee | 1958

This was a piece of classic atmospheric pop from the sultry songstress Peggy Lee, its witty lyrics faultlessly arranged and perfectly delivered—"What a lovely way to burn."

Winter Wonderland
Darlene Love | 1963

Each December in Manhattan, Phil Spector's Christmas Album from 1963 can be heard everywhere, from high-end department stores to supermarkets to Santa Claus collecting for charity on the street corners. Darlene Love sang four memorable tracks on the album, including this wonderful version of a Christmas classic; "Sleigh bells ring, are you listening?"

Stuck in the Middle with You
Louise | 2001

This may be blasphemy to many, but I actually prefer this modern R&B take on the Stealers Wheel 1973 classic—and the singer's better looking too!

Hippy Hippy Shake
The Swinging Blue Jeans | 1963

A powerful cover of the Chan Romero original, this was the epitome of the "Liverpool Sound"—if there really was such a thing—that was heralded in the charts by The Beatles.

Hey! Baby
Bruce Channel | 1962

This is the record that is said to have inspired John Lennon to include the harmonica on The Beatles' debut disc "Love Me Do," and it is also a piece of solid early '60s pop in its own right.

Never Ever
All Saints | 1997

After the Spice Girls became the biggest thing in pop in 1996, flaunting feminine mayhem on a dozen kids' TV shows and calling it "Girl Power," along came All Saints, sassy, grown-up, genuinely sexy—and that was just "Never Ever." Never again equaled by Natalie and Nicole Appleton, Melanie Blatt, and the song's composer Shaznay Lewis, but a thing of wonder all the same, this track is a real spine tingler.

Sweets for My Sweet
The Searchers | 1963

The Searchers from Liverpool, England were one of the most polished groups to emerge in the wake of The Beatles. Their fine version of this Drifters original was, like The Beatles' covers, no mere imitation.

Move It
Cliff Richard | 1958

Although he mellowed fairly swiftly, veteran British rocker Cliff Richard's debut single was potent stuff, with a guitar intro that resonates even today.

You Are the Sunshine of My Life
Stevie Wonder | 1972

A standard of the '70s, this upbeat Grammy Award-winning love song was Stevie Wonder's most complete crossover into the pop mainstream, and his most successful.

A Whiter Shade of Pale
Procol Harum | 1967

Evoking the spirit of the "Summer of Love" like few other records of its time, the cod-surrealist lyrics—"We skipped the light fandango, turned cartwheels 'cross the floor"—and Bach quotes on the organ added up to classic psychedelia. Trippy, hippie, and, ultimately, a little dippy, but utterly memorable.

Tutti Frutti
Little Richard | 1955

Together with his 1956 hit "Long Tall Sally," this track could be said to define early rock-'n'-roll and it became a model for many of Little Richard's future songs. It also has the greatest intro lyric in pop history: "A wop bop a loo bop a lop bam boom!"

Do Wah Diddy Diddy
Manfred Mann | 1964

A marvelous slice of nonsense pop that, unlike much British beat boom material circa 1964, has remained oddly memorable, "...dum diddy do!"

Mull of Kintyre
Paul McCartney | 1977

Paul McCartney's songwriting skills have been applied to many diverse styles of song. Written with the help of Denny Laine, this huge-selling evocation (complete with bagpipe chorus) of the Scottish coastland where he had a farm, was just one of McCartney's many successes.

Sugar Sugar
The Archies | 1969

The ultimate manufactured band, the Archies were an animated music group that featured in the successful Saturday morning children's cartoon *Archie*. The studio musicians behind the animated characters were put together by Don Kirshner, creator of The Monkees, for this slice of pure bubblegum.

Runaway
Del Shannon | 1961

With the echo effect on the Musitron (a type of electronic organ) turned up full, Del Shannon's strident vocals made this a song of anguish to remember.

Mack the Knife
Bobby Darin | 1959

A roaring production in which smooth, finger-clickin' Darin had the edge on every other version (including those by Ella Fitzgerald and Louis Armstrong) of this tremendous Bertolt Brecht and Kurt Weill song from *The Threepenny Opera*.

Pray
Take That | 1993

Boy bands (though how the term "band" ever came to refer to purely vocal groups is one of life's mysteries) have been a genuine pop phenomenon of the '90s and '00s, and Take That were the original article. "Pray" was their first in no less than eight U.K. chart toppers before they finally disbanded in 1996.

I Got You Babe
Sonny and Cher | 1965

Producer Sonny Bono came up with this timeless hit on the crest of the U.S. folk-rock scene. He and partner Cher coyly looked into each other's eyes as they sang this on countless TV pop shows worldwide accompanied by that insistent oboe in the chorus.

Catch a Falling Star
Perry Como | 1958

Smooth-voiced baritone Perry Como was the archetypal middle-of-
the-road singer, who made pure pop records with professional ease
and style. "Catch a Falling Star" was a U.S. chart topper that also
earned him a Grammy for Best Male Vocalist, whereas the song's
flip side "Magic Moments" went to Number One in the U.K. charts.

Anyone Who Had a Heart
Cilla Black | 1964

Written by Burt Bacharach and Hal David, this is a surprisingly
sensitive version of Dionne Warwick's U.S. hit, especially
considering Cilla's usually strident delivery in the mezzo-soprano
range. George Martin—sometimes known as "the fifth Beatle"—
produced, which probably says a lot.

Big Girls Don't Cry
The Four Seasons | 1962

Frankie Valli's amazing falsetto made the refined doo-wop of The
Four Seasons instantly recognizable—one of *the* sounds of the '60s.

No Scrubs
TLC | 1999

R&B meets classy pop on this general dis of lazy, loser guys—
they're the "scrubs" of the title—from one of the biggest-selling and
most sadly-missed female groups of the '90s. This was one of the
many superlative tracks from Atlanta's T-Boz, Left-Eye, and Chilli—
hence TLC, geddit?

California Dreamin'
The Mamas and The Papas | 1966

"All the leaves are brown, and the sky is gray..." so begins this wintertime anthem to the warm allure of the West Coast. This is an utterly unforgettable, well-crafted, and uplifting prediction of the hippie dream.

Heart of Glass
Blondie | 1979

"Once I had a love and it was a gas, soon turned out to be a pain in the ass"—in every sense of the word, this was Blondie's greatest hit. Perfectly written, perfectly pitched, perfectly arranged, perfectly crafted, perfectly recorded. Perfect pop.

Da Doo Ron Ron
The Crystals | 1963

A tremendously popular hit (despite the ever-changing lineup of this successful girl group) that was the epitome of influential producer Phil Spector's multilayered "Wall of Sound" technique back in the days of mono recordings.

Girls and Boys
Blur | 1994

Blur were at the forefront of the Britpop movement that shook up the U.K. music scene in the mid '90s. "Girls and Boys" was the track that frantically heralded their chart success, which continued throughout the latter half of the decade.

Wake Up Little Susie
The Everly Brothers | 1957

Country rock of an early kind, the hard-edged harmonies of The Everly Brothers were brought to bear on a series of huge hits that put Nashville on the rock-'n'-roll map for the very first time. This controversial track was their first Number One.

Yesterday Once More
The Carpenters | 1973

Their popularity baffled the critics and many found this brother and sister vocal group's wholesome image more than a little hard to take, but their equally clean-cut sound was an essential part of the soundtrack of the '70s.

Hello Mary Lou
Rick Nelson | 1961

Late '50s and early '60s teenage heartthrob Rick Nelson made some fine rockabilly-influenced singles. Guitarist James Burton shines through on this strong Gene Pitney-penned track that was released as the flipside to "Travelin' Man."

...Baby One More Time
Britney Spears | 1998

Despite the moral outrage—or perhaps partly because of it—Britney Spears's "schoolgirl" video for her chart-topping debut single, "...Baby One More Time," certainly helped catapult the then 15-year-old into pop's top class.

I Want It That Way
Backstreet Boys | 1999

Charting thanks to airplay alone in the U.S., this is ultimate Backstreet Boys—the band that took boy bands into a new era with classic vocals on top of super-chunky production. This track saw Kevin, Brian, Howard, AJ, and Nick at the top of their game, having earned success throughout Europe and Canada before finally cracking the States.

Great Balls of Fire
Jerry Lee Lewis | 1957

Goodness gracious! A pumping piano thumper in the midst of rockabilly guitarists, wild man Jerry Lee Lewis was undoubtedly one of the greatest graduates of Sam Phillips' Sun Studios in Memphis, Tennessee.

I Just Don't Know What to Do with Myself
Dusty Springfield | 1964

A classic Burt Bacharach and Hal David song from one of their foremost interpreters—a dramatic orchestration always brought out the best in Dusty.

Sailing
Rod Stewart | 1975

A sing-along anthem that was one of the gravelly-voiced singer's biggest hits, "Sailing" has been a staple of flag-waving troopship farewells ever since.

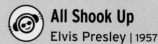

All Shook Up
Elvis Presley | 1957

There are a handful of records scattered throughout these pages
that are the ultimate in pop perfection. Perfectly written, arranged,
engineered, produced, and performed, yet they must also have that
indefinable something that puts them in a league of their own.
Elvis's sixth chart topper is one of those songs.

There Must Be an Angel
(Playing With My Heart)
Eurythmics | 1985

Annie Lennox's blue-eyed soul shines through on this track that
even includes an uncredited harmonica contribution from Stevie
Wonder. Despite the rather obvious pun, there's simply no other
word to describe this, but heavenly.

It's in His Kiss
Betty Everett | 1964

Also known and sometimes released as "The Shoop Shoop Song,"
this tune was successfully revived by Linda Lewis in 1975 and again
by Cher in 1990, but neither of them matched Everett's classic
forthright interpretation.

Freak Like Me
Sugababes | 2002

All-girl pop dance group Sugababes were part of the feminine
flipside of the "boy band" bonanza, and "Freak Like Me" was their
first Number One, with samples from Gary Numan in the mix.

Peggy Sue
Buddy Holly | 1957

With Jerry Allison's memorably frenetic drum intro, this was the record that really introduced Buddy Holly to the charts. He had actually been there a few months earlier, as part of The Crickets (who were still backing him here) with another of his most famous singles "That'll Be the Day."

Shakin' All Over
Johnny Kidd and the Pirates | 1960

A British pop masterpiece that aimed to send "quivers down my backbone..." by equating rock-'n'-roll with raw sex. Perhaps something everyone needed reminding of in 1960, what with Elvis in the army and Cliff Richard and the Shadows ruling the charts.

Sweet Nothin's
Brenda Lee | 1959

With a tough-sounding adult voice at odds with her youthful image and diminutive size, teen idol Brenda Lee—who earned the nickname "Little Miss Dynamite"—was only 15 years old when this knowingly suggestive single hit the charts, "My baby whispers in my ear..."

Tug of War
Paul McCartney | 1982

Certainly one of McCartney's most accomplished tracks in his long, but often patchy, post-Beatles career, this single came from his acclaimed album of the same name. Simply marvelous.

Make It Easy on Yourself
The Walker Brothers | 1965

Scott Walker's dramatic delivery and the Brothers' ambitious Phil Spector-influenced productions distinguished their few but memorable hits, especially this grandiose take on a classic Burt Bacharach and Hal David song.

Merry Xmas Everybody
Slade | 1973

This is another record that you just can't get away from during the holiday season. Glam rock band Slade topped the U.K. charts with this festive single in 1973 and they've been dining off the proceeds ever since.

Downtown
Petula Clark | 1964

Pure-voiced Pet was a teenage star in England before breaking into the international market in a big way with this hit. Her best-remembered single, this was her first American Number One and it won her a Grammy Award.

Thriller
Michael Jackson | 1983

Although never quite justifying his publicity machine's description of him as "The King of Pop," Michael Jackson has sold millions and millions of records. "Thriller," with an ambitious horror-film music video as its promotional centerpiece, was the biggest of them all.

It's Over
Roy Orbison | 1964

"The Big O" went a tad over the top on many of his records, but despite the histrionics, he made some classic pop ballads in the early '60s that owed much to his rockabilly background.

Think It Over
Buddy Holly | 1958

With a raunchy piano solo from producer Norman Petty where you might have expected a guitar, this tough-sounding track from Buddy Holly confirmed that, despite some "pretty" hits, he was a rock-'n'-roller at heart.

Mis-Shapes / Sorted for E's & Wizz
Pulp | 1995

Gritty, camp, and melancholic, this style of pop could only emerge from the U.K. This was a double A-side, with one side ("Mis-shapes") melancholic and the other ("Sorted for E's & Whizz") fueling a major tabloid controversy over its lyrics. Neither song did any harm in propelling the album *Different Class* to the heights of the U.K. album charts.

(There's) Always Something There to Remind Me
Sandie Shaw | 1964

The English exponent of the American soft-soul style of the mid '60s, bare-footed Sandie Shaw had her first hit with a great version of this Burt Bacharach and Hal David song.

Here Comes Summer
Jerry Keller | 1959

This was Keller's only real triumph as a singer, although he went on to have a very successful songwriting career. It was one of 1959's biggest summer hits—school's out, vacation's starting, the days are long and warm, "Here comes summertime at last..."

King Midas in Reverse
The Hollies | 1967

One of the slicker groups to come out of The Beatles-led beat boom in Britain in '63, Manchester's The Hollies' finest hour came in the psychedelic years of '66-67. "King Midas" leans towards over-production in places, as did much post *Sgt. Pepper* pop in '67, but it is beautifully crafted and very much of its time.

Make Me Smile (Come Up and See Me)
Steve Harley and Cockney Rebel | 1975

Steve Harley struggled to convince the world of the "serious" side to his glam-oriented group, all to no avail. But this song still resonates as an echo of pre-punk pop and has become hugely popular, featuring in countless TV and radio advertising campaigns and apparently being covered more than 100 times!

YMCA
The Village People | 1978

Annoying maybe, but a true (and not just gay) anthem all the same. This joyful kitsch pop song for sing-along party people everywhere still gets them moving on the dance floor with its cheerleader-style dance and chant: "Young man, there's a place you can go..."

Breaking Up Is Hard to Do
Neil Sedaka | 1962

As a songwriter, Sedaka provided some potent hits for a variety of singers, while his own output as a vocalist was, in the main, fairly lightweight. Nevertheless, songs like "Oh Carol," "Happy Birthday Sweet Sixteen," and "Breaking Up Is Hard to Do," were pure unpretentious pop, perfectly executed.

The Tide Is High
Blondie | 1980

This reggae-tinged number was originally written by John Holt of Jamaican band The Paragons in the mid '60s. It became a perfect, although unlikely, vehicle for Blondie lead singer Debbie Harry's languid vocals combined with some burning brass arrangements.

Can't Get You Out of My Head
Kylie Minogue | 2001

Nineties dance diva Cathy Dennis and former Mud band member Rob Davis penned pure pop perfection for Australia's favorite micro pop princess. The unforgettable chant of "na-na-na-na" and a futuristic music video shot Kylie to the top of the charts in more than 30 countries throughout the world.

ROCK SOLID

After the rock-'n'-roll revolution of the 1950s, popular music was never the same again. Throughout the subsequent decades, a solid body of rock-based music developed that simply would not have existed otherwise. Country rock, folk rock, psychedelic rock, blues-based rock, punk rock, pub rock, indie rock, soft rock, and hard rock—not to mention power pop, Britpop, and heavy metal—all evolved from the musical "Big Bang" ignited by Elvis and the rest. Rock on!

Born to Run
Bruce Springsteen | 1975

New Jersey's Bruce Springsteen was declared the great new hope of rock music when he burst onto the scene in the '70s. His no-nonsense brand of rock-'n'-roll certainly came as an antidote to the increasingly pretentious "progressive" bands and later, the often musically inept punks.

The Joshua Tree
U2 | 1987

This crowd-pleasing Irish rock band became worldwide stadium superstars in the '80s—*The Joshua Tree* was pivotal in that change. It is their most successful album to date, topping the album charts in the U.S. and the U.K. and winning a Grammy Award for Album of the Year.

Light My Fire
The Doors | 1967

Would-be poet Jim Morrison and the group never seemed sure whether they were a pop-influenced psychedelic group or vice versa. Commercially, with guitarist Robbie Krieger's "Light My Fire," pop won the day—but don't say that to die-hard Morrison freaks!

KC Jones (on the Road Again)
North Mississippi Allstars | 2000

The old folk legend of railroad man Casey Jones—written and released as "Kassie Jones" by the great blues musician Furry Lewis in the late '20s—raised its head yet again courtesy of funky three-piece blues-rock band the North Mississippi Allstars.

Bohemian Rhapsody
Queen | 1975

Freddie Mercury and the boys' greatest achievement in their typically over-the-top style was a six-minute epic that threw together hard rock, heavy metal, and balladeering histrionics. Though few of us can recite the lyrics, once it starts playing we all just join in instinctively, like it or not. "Galileo, Galileo..."

Yeah Yeah Yeahs
Yeah Yeah Yeahs | 2001

The raw energy vocals of lead singer Karen O, combined with crackling guitar and blistering jazz-driven drumming, put the Yeah Yeah Yeahs' debut EP at the cutting edge of early twenty-first-century indie punk rock.

Highway 61 Revisited
Dr. Feelgood | 1987

English pub rockers Dr. Feelgood gave us this echo-rich, hard-driving version of Bob Dylan's unforgettable 1965 single on their 1987 album, which was simply called *Classic*.

Destroyer
Kiss | 1976

At the cartoon-character end of pomp-rock—the band actually had a Marvel comic based on them at one stage—Kiss were famous for their elaborate makeup and over-the-top stage presentations. Having said that, they also had a huge influence on just about every American heavy rock band of the '80s and '90s. *Destroyer* was their most successful album.

You Wear It Well
Rod Stewart | 1972

Before leaving the Faces to go solo, Rod Stewart released a couple
of crucial albums under his own name, but with the band—and
others—backing. The second album, *Never a Dull Moment*, included
this U.K. Number One hit single, which immediately became a major
item in the Stewart canon.

Appetite for Destruction
Guns n' Roses | 1987

Aptly named, the 'Roses biggest-selling album was a no-holds-
barred celebration of sex, drugs, and rock-'n'-roll.

Southside
Texas | 1988

The modern guitar-led soul of this Scottish rock group fronted by
singer and guitarist Sharleen Spiteri was first heard on their fine
debut album *Southside*, which included their first hit single "I Don't
Want a Lover."

Blood, Sweat and Tears
Blood, Sweat and Tears | 1968

From a pioneering attempt at jazz-rock fusion, Blood, Sweat and
Tears evolved into a mainstream rock act with predictable
arrangements and strident—but equally characterless—vocals by
David Clayton-Thomas. Their eponymous 1968 album caught them
at their creative peak and, as well as charting itself, produced three
million-selling singles: "You've Made Me So Very Happy," "And When
I Die," and "Spinning Wheel."

He's on the Phone

Saint Etienne | 1995

Originally predating the Britpop boom by a couple of years, Saint Etienne's melodic, danceable music and Sarah Cracknell's solid vocalizing hit their commercial peak just when Oasis and Blur were battling it out in the charts. Nevertheless, they were one of the best outfits of the early '90s.

House of the Rising Sun

The Animals | 1964

Allegedly the single that convinced Bob Dylan to "go electric," this British R&B cover of an old American folk ballad was taken from Dylan's own debut album. The Animals changed the lyrics slightly, making the central character male, so they didn't have to sing as a "poor girl" the way Dylan did.

Blood Sugar Sex Magik

Red Hot Chili Peppers | 1991

Red hot and rocking, the Chili's have purveyed a potent mix of funk, punk, and metal-hard rock for over 20 years—and are still going strong. Their pivotal album *Blood Sugar Sex Magik* sold more than seven million copies worldwide.

Rockin' All over the World

Status Quo | 1977

British denim rockers Status Quo memorably opened the Live Aid concerts at Wembley Stadium, London in 1985 with this track; after that, what was just one of their many straightforward hits soon became a genuine rock-'n'-roll anthem.

Denis
Blondie | 1978

"I've got a crush on you," sang Debbie Harry on Blondie's debut hit—although their debut album, simply entitled *Blondie*, had already been released in 1977—and most of the male population answered likewise. She could do it in French, too!

Murmur
R.E.M. | 1983

Critically-acclaimed and influential rock group R.E.M. took indie music into the mainstream with a vengeance when they released *Murmur*. With its strong melodies and purposeful lyrics, this was truly a landmark album in '80s rock.

Guitar Man
Bread | 1972

Soft rock or sophisticated pop, call it whatever you like, but David Gates' quartet defined smooth easy listening with a clutch of hits in the early '70s, including this popular track from the album of the same name.

Seven Nation Army
The White Stripes | 2003

With possibly the most maddeningly catchy hook of recent times, "Seven Nation Army" was always going to be huge. It united rockers and dance-bunnies alike with its minimalist rock-'n'-roll simplicity and upbeat raw garage energy, while The White Stripes duo titillated the world with the enigma of whether they are brother and sister or a divorced couple.

Brass in Pocket
The Pretenders | 1979

American singer, songwriter, and musician Chrissie Hynde fronted British New Wave band The Pretenders in the wake of punk with a classic self-named debut album best remembered for this hit single. This was effortless, slightly world-weary rock completely of its time—"special, so special..."

Master of Puppets
Metallica | 1986

Archetypal thrash-metal band Metallica injected heavy metal with a punk dynamic with heady—or perhaps headbanging—results. Though some of their later albums sold far more copies, *Master of Puppets* was undoubtedly the band's finest hour.

Whole Lotta Love
Led Zeppelin | 1969

With a guitar riff that became anthemic in itself, this track from the godfathers of heavy metal Led Zeppelin, when their sound was still just seen as the loud end of the British blues boom, was their biggest American hit single.

Cigarettes and Alcohol
Oasis | 1994

Probably penned under the influence of both of these obsessions, this homage to the simple pleasures of the working man is a heady mix of all that is good about Oasis—Liam Gallagher's snarled vocals, his brother Noel's post-punk pop-rock melodies, and a collective nod to The Beatles.

Rumours
Fleetwood Mac | 1976

Starting off as a straight-down-the-line British blues band, the Mac grew into the biggest act in mainstream rock of their era. The mega-selling *Rumours* album was undoubtedly their finest hour, reflecting almost confessionally on the real-life affairs between members of the group.

The Paul Butterfield Blues Band
The Paul Butterfield Blues Band | 1965

Singer and harmonica player Paul Butterfield and guitarists Michael Bloomfield and Elvin Bishop were catalysts in the development of electric rock. This breakthrough album was followed by their backing Bob Dylan's first electric performance at the 1965 Newport Folk Festival. Vital stuff.

The Head on the Door
The Cure | 1985

In the wake of punk proper, Robert Smith's gothic-pop band were cult favorites throughout the late '70s and early '80s. More commercial than some of their earlier offerings, this sixth album—released by a much-altered lineup—was their first to crack the U.S. album charts and it remains one of their most popular.

All Right Now
Free | 1970

This British blues-rock anthem had earthy vocals, soaring guitar, and a rock-solid rhythm section—"There she stood in the street, smilin' from her head to her feet..."

Yellow

Coldplay | 2000

Probably the best-behaved rock stars in the world, Coldplay are synonymous with those achingly catchy, resolutely middle-of-the-road ditties that even your Grandma would like. Taken from their multi-platinum album *Parachutes*, "Yellow" has a thread of melancholy running through it that pushes the song into heart-wrenching territory.

The Price of Love

Bryan Ferry | 1976

Horn-driven riffs—plus some sexy yelping from the foxy backing vocalists—drive this powerful version of a mid '60s Everly Brothers hit by British singer Bryan Ferry, who first gained fame as the lead vocalist of Roxy Music.

The Number of the Beast

Iron Maiden | 1982

Described by one writer as "a cultural touchstone for the term heavy metal," British band Iron Maiden did indeed define the genre as it was evolving into its second wave in the '80s with the release of this crucial album.

Hi Ho Silver Lining

Jeff Beck | 1967

Blues and rock guitar ace Jeff Beck made some uncharacteristic singles in the late '60s, including this odd chant against fake hippies which hooked everyone with its sing-along chorus: "You're everywhere and nowhere, baby, that's where you're at…"

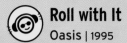

Roll with It
Oasis | 1995

At the height of the Britpop boom, Mancunian rockers Oasis were at their peak. This is perhaps the best in a series of multi-layered, psychedelic-edged pop records that captured the spirit of the time perfectly, but with a retro glance.

Stay with Me
Faces | 1972

When Mod group The Small Faces split up, the remains evolved into the Faces, with like-minded Rod Stewart (who was known as "Rod the Mod" in the '60s) joining them on some good-time vocals. "Stay With Me" was the band's only American Top 40 hit.

Endsongs
Longwave | 2000

Critically acclaimed as one of the best bands to come out of New York in several years, Longwave's debut album combined strong melodies and intelligent lyrics, drawing comparisons with the guitar-oriented band Radiohead.

Ball and Chain
Janis Joplin / Big Brother and the
Holding Company | 1968

A high point of the Monterey Pop Festival in June 1967, Janis Joplin's rough-at-the-edges blues voice memorably repeated her raw interpretation of Willie Mae Thornton's "Ball and Chain" on the *Cheap Thrills* album the following year.

Slippery When Wet
Bon Jovi | 1986

Taking a populist attitude to stadium rock dynamics, Bon Jovi managed to sell heavy metal to the masses in quantities other bands had only dreamed of. *Slippery When Wet* earned no less than ten platinum discs, with two U.S. chart toppers—"You Give Love a Bad Name" and "Livin' on a Prayer"—spun off as singles.

Rocky Mountain Way
Joe Walsh | 1973

From his annoyingly-titled second album *The Smoker You Drink, The Player You Get*, this is a memorably powerful piece of slide guitar hard rock from Walsh. It was also his biggest hit before joining the Eagles as a replacement for Bernie Leadon in 1975.

You Really Got Me
The Kinks | 1964

"Oh yeah..." Classic Brit-beat R&B from the influential rockers led by brothers Ray and Dave Davies. With a two-chord guitar riff, frantic soloing, and in-your-face vocals, this track was the punk rock of its day.

Acme
Jon Spencer Blues Explosion | 1998

Originally part of New York's alternative rock scene, Spencer and his band went on to explore the music's ancestral roots in country blues with this album, albeit in a thoroughly modern context with elements of electronic rock and hip hop thrown into the mix, too.

Last Nite
The Strokes | 2001

"Last Nite" was one of the standout tracks on the much-hyped debut album, *Is This It*, by New York rock band The Strokes. Though the band have yet to follow through as many expected, the album still shines as a fine example of the band's melodic guitar-led pop that offered a much-needed breath of fresh air at the time.

Band on the Run
Paul McCartney | 1973

After a rather shaky start following the breakup of the biggest pop group in music history, *Band on the Run* is the album that firmly established that Paul McCartney, as a songwriter and performer par excellence, was back!

Rocket Man
Elton John | 1972

The combination of Elton John's melodies and Bernie Taupin's lyrical skill, often wasted on less substantial material, was at its most potent on this song: "I think it's gonna be a long, long time..."

Firestarter
The Prodigy | 1996

An outrageous image combined with a white-heat guitar sound and manic vocals–"I'm the self-inflicted, punk detonator"–catapulted The Prodigy's demonic single to the top of the U.K. charts. This success came despite, or perhaps partly because, the video was nearly banned following criticism of its arson obsession from the tabloid newspapers.

The Captain and Me
The Doobie Brothers | 1973

With memorable tracks including the hits "China Grove" and "Long Train Runnin'," the Doobie's most accomplished album was a perfect example of how mainstream American rock had seamlessly absorbed country, blues, and folk music by the early '70s.

Out of Time
Chris Farlowe | 1966

Written by the Rolling Stones and produced by Mick Jagger, this one-off U.K. chart topper for gritty-voiced Farlowe may sound a little dated on the surface, but is still impressive at its core: "Well, baby, baby, baby..."

Money for Nothing
Dire Straits | 1985

Mark Knopfler's seamlessly perfect guitar playing and Dylanesque vocals gelled into some fine tracks by the oft-maligned 'Straits, which he co-led with his brother David. "Money for Nothing," which featured Sting singing the introduction and backing chorus, was Dire Straits' only American Number One single.

Tales from Topographic Oceans
Yes | 1973

Arguably the most overambitious of the "classical rock" bands that were at the core of the early '70s progressive scene, Yes' *Tales from Topographic Oceans* was a symphonic concept album based on Indian scriptures. It marked a watershed in rock when the music had to change or disappear into its own navel-gazing.

I Am the Walrus
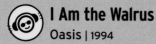
Oasis | 1994

The flipside to the Gallagher brothers' single "Cigarettes and Alcohol," this was a mind-blowing reworking of their hero John Lennon's masterpiece of pop surrealism: "I am he as you are he."

The Allman Brothers Band

The Allman Brothers Band | 1969

A blues-flavored Southern rock band, the Allmans' eponymous debut album ensured their place on rock festival bills throughout the early '70s. Although it was not a big-seller, the album gave the band critical acclaim and a cult following, and was an inspiration to the other down-home boogie bands that followed.

Come On Eileen

Dexy's Midnight Runners | 1982

This sing-along favorite from the Irish-influenced rock-'n'-soul group went to Number One in the U.S. and the U.K.—and was even the biggest-selling U.K. single of the year. Come on, everybody, "Toora loo rye aye..."

Paranoid

Black Sabbath | 1970

Founding figures in heavy rock, Ozzy Osbourne and the boys came out of the same British blues scene as their contemporaries—and early rivals—Led Zeppelin. Their second album, *Paranoid*, proved to be a primer in what heavy metal was all about.

Whatcha Gonna Do About It
The Small Faces | 1965

Although this diminutive British Mod band earned more critical acclaim when they moved into their "psychedelic" period, their first hit "Whatcha Gonna Do About It" remains their finest as the preeminent group of "faces" in '60s Swinging London.

Dark Side of the Moon
Pink Floyd | 1973

Doom-ridden, certainly, but this was also a massive-selling landmark album (over 35 million copies sold worldwide to date). It tapped into the early '70s progressive rock market that, like the Floyd themselves, evolved directly out of '60s psychedelia.

Living in the USA
The Steve Miller Band | 1968

With a driving harmonica reminiscent of the band's earlier days playing at the Avalon Ballroom as The Steve Miller Blues Band, this chart entry single was the first hit culled from the *Sailor* album, a classic of the psychedelic era.

Traveling Wilburys, Vol. 1
Traveling Wilburys | 1988

The all-star lineup of Bob Dylan, Roy Orbison, Tom Petty, George Harrison, and Jeff Lynne couldn't really go wrong—and they didn't! They had two best-selling albums, including this their highly-acclaimed debut, and a clutch of hit singles to prove it.

 Tommy
The Who | 1969

Tommy was the first and, to this day, one of the few successful attempts at a rock opera. As with all good musicals, the strength of *Tommy* lay in the quality of the individual songs. In that respect, it couldn't fail—"The Acid Queen," "It's a Boy," "Pinball Wizard," "Tommy Can You Hear Me?" and the rest, make for a heady score.

Delta Lady
Leon Russell | 1970

All-round multi-instrumentalist, writer, and producer Leon Russell sings this evocative love song dedicated to Rita Coolidge, which he originally wrote for Joe Cocker. It comes from Russell's self-titled album, for which he gathered together an all-star lineup that included Steve Winwood, Eric Clapton, Ringo Starr, Bill Wyman, and George Harrison,

All You Good Good People
Embrace | 1997

With the inevitable comparisons to Oasis and The Verve ringing in their ears, British band Embrace leaped from the shadows of both to release this gutsy anthem, becoming a minor rock-sensation in the U.K. and firm favorites on American college radio.

Highway to Hell
AC/DC | 1979

Produced by Robert "Mutt" Lange, this was the first million-selling album from the Australian hard rockers AC/DC. It was also the final album with the original AC/DC lineup—lead singer Bon Scott tragically died in 1980.

Gimme Some Lovin'
The Spencer Davis Group | 1966

Out of the British R&B boom, The Spencer Davis Group was instrumental in launching the then-precocious Ray Charles sound-alike Steve Winwood on an amazed public. This track was their best.

Trash
[The London] Suede | 1996

Possibly the sexiest ensemble to emerge from the U.K. in the '90s, Brett Anderson and co. were hailed as rock *wunderkinds* before they'd even sold a note. With androgynous Anderson penning such post-Britpop perfection as this track—with its glam-era David Bowie kick—chart domination was assured.

Changes
David Bowie | 1971

From his *Hunky Dory* album of 1971, this was a major Bowie theme that offered a foretaste of his masterpiece album *The Rise and Fall of Ziggy Stardust and the Spiders from Mars* that was to be released the following year.

The Adventures of Grandmaster Flash on the Wheels of Steel
Grandmaster Flash | 1981

With excerpts from the likes of Chic, Blondie, Queen, and rappers the Sugarhill Gang, this offering from Grandmaster Flash was one of the first examples of DJ mixing and scratching, and it is still regarded as possibly the finest recorded example of what is essentially a "live" genre.

With a Little Help from My Friends
Joe Cocker | 1968

Joe Cocker's career really took off when he sang this at Woodstock in 1969. It is one of the most successful re-workings of any Beatles' number and, stylistically, a million miles from the original. Riveting.

Sheer Heart Attack
Queen | 1974

Preluding their monumental album *A Night at the Opera*, which had "Bohemian Rhapsody" as its remarkable centerpiece, was this third album by Queen. It was their most solid foray into the pre-punk rock market and many longtime fans still consider it as May, Mercury, Deacon, and Taylor at their very best.

Groovin'
The Young Rascals | 1967

"Groovin' on a Sunday afternoon..." along with The Young Rascals (aka The Rascals) who, together with The Lovin' Spoonful, became the New York soundtrack to summer in the city in the late '60s.

Too Long in Exile
Van Morrison | 1993

A wonderful album by the always remarkable Morrison, with his versions of jazz, R&B, and soul classics, including "Lonely Avenue," "Ball & Chain," "Good Morning Little Schoolgirl," and "Moody's Mood for Love" which were all equal to—but never bettered—the sensational title track.

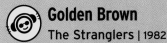

Golden Brown
The Stranglers | 1982

Though the lyrics are actually about heroin, this song—written by
the band's lead singer Hugh Cornwell—has a lilting, waltz-time
melody far removed from its grim subject. "Never a frown..."

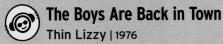

The Boys Are Back in Town
Thin Lizzy | 1976

The Irish rockers' biggest-selling single in the U.S., this track from
the album *Jailbreak* is still Thin Lizzy's best-known song—an
anthemic hit from Phil Lynott's hard-rocking good-time boys.

Our House
Madness | 1982

British ska band Madness brought a reggae "rude boy" ambience to
the kind of working-class nostalgia also found in the lyrics of Ray
Davies and Ian Dury. This track was the essential '80s right "in the
middle of our street."

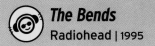

The Bends
Radiohead | 1995

A flawless, perhaps even a little too polished, collection from the
modern-day standard bearers of "progressive" rock, in the best
sense of the word. With soaring vocals, incisive playing, and just a
touch of the experimentation that would inform their later work,
this album was a minor masterpiece.

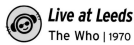

Live at Leeds
The Who | 1970

The live album that established The Who not just as Mod maestros playing Pete Townshend's originals, but rockers perfectly capable of tackling vintage material ranging from Johnny Kidd's "Shakin' All Over" and Eddie Cochran's "Summertime Blues" to Mose Allison's idiosyncratic "Young Man Blues."

Bad Moon Rising
Creedence Clearwater Revival | 1969

"Bad Moon Rising" was a million-selling slice of revisionist rockabilly from one of the biggest American bands of the late '60s and early '70s.

Eliminator
ZZ Top | 1983

Bearded—except for drummer Frank Beard who was, ironically, clean-shaven—Texan rockers ZZ Top played straight down-the-line heavy blues laced rock with, after this milestone album, hints of disco and out-and-out pop.

Uptown Girl
Billy Joel | 1983

The exclamatory "Uptown Girl" epitomized Joel's forthright style and paid homage to Frankie Valli and the Four Seasons. Joel's wife-to-be at that time, the model Christy Brinkley, also memorably appeared as the infamous uptown girl of the title in the song's garage mechanic music video.

Rocks
Aerosmith | 1976

One of the first wave of heavy metal bands, Aerosmith's finest hour came in 1976 with their fourth album, *Rocks*. From the album's opening track "Back in the Saddle" to the final "Home Tonight," you know you've been truly rocked by vocalist Steve Tyler and the rest of the gang.

Disraeli Gears
Cream | 1967

This is the album that made Cream a supergroup, with Eric Clapton, Jack Bruce, and Ginger Baker all at the very height of their powers. Awesome psychedelic blues—including the sublime single "Sunshine of Your Love"—before the band OD'd on mammoth live performances.

Astro Creep: 2000 Songs of Love, Destruction, and Other Synthetic Delusions of the Electric Head
White Zombie | 1995

Bringing a heavy metal dynamic to the New York underground club circuit, Rob Zombie's band was a virtually unique link between alternative art-noise rock and mainstream metal. The portentously-named album *Astro Creep: 2000...* was a million-selling testament to this crossover.

Dance On

Dancing has been linked to music since the dawn of time. From the waltz, through early fads like the tango and Charleston, to the Lindy Hop, the Twist, and disco dancing, popular music has constantly been at the service of the world's flappers and gliders, boppers and jivers. Dance craze records, from exotic sambas, mambos, and congas to doin' the funky chicken and walkin' the dog, have often outlasted the dances themselves and the drama of the dance floor, with its wallflowers, dancing queens, and last dance romances, has been a constant theme for songwriters. Like the man said, it's time to get down and boogie!

Let's Twist Again
Chubby Checker | 1961

"Like we did last summer..." The Twist was one of *the* great dance crazes—and the one ideal for people who couldn't actually dance! The dance's greatest hit was in this follow-up to "The Twist" from the year before.

Mambo No. 5
Lou Bega | 1999

The mambo—a Latin-American dance fad from the early '50s, which was swiftly succeeded by the cha cha cha—enjoyed a surprise revival in the late '90s when German singer Bega added lyrics to a 1952 instrumental by the original mambo master Pérez Prado.

The Loco-Motion
Little Eva | 1962

"Everybody's doin' a brand-new dance..." after husband-and-wife songwriting team Gerry Goffin and Carole King recruited their daughter's babysitter Eva Boyd for this novelty dance that became a fondly-remembered smash hit.

Jive Talkin'
The Bee Gees | 1975

Moving on from their earlier, clean-cut, ballad-singing incarnation, this single heralded the arrival of a much more exciting product from the brothers Gibb. A U.S. Number One for them, this stuttery disco track was their first flirtation with disco and white satin suits—a new image that paid off for them time and time again throughout the disco decade.

Walk Like an Egyptian
The Bangles | 1986

Quintessential all-girl '80s group The Bangles had a worldwide hit with this quirky but funky single, which took people straight onto the dance floor with their arms in the air, doing the Ancient Egyptians' "sand dance." The Bangles at their best.

The Stroll
The Diamonds | 1958

Hot on the heels of their 1957 hit "Little Darlin'," The Diamonds strolled into the U.S. Top Five again with the release of this doo-wop song in response to a typically short-lived dance craze.

I Feel Love
Donna Summer | 1977

With this pared-down disco number, Summer brought the world its first pop hit to boast an entirely synthesized backing track, which came courtesy of producers Giorgio Moroder and Pete Bellotte. The techno craze of the '80s and '90s—not to mention many weird European dance "hits" since—can be traced back to this tune. It still sounds as good as it ever did.

Praise You
Fatboy Slim | 1998

Former Housemartin Norman Cook (aka Fatboy Slim) pioneered the dance music style dubbed "big beat" on this breakthrough track. Its phenomenal success on both sides of the Pond owed as much to its catchiness as it did to its off-the-wall video directed by Spike Jonze, which won three MTV Video Awards.

Honky Tonk Women

Rolling Stones | 1969

A Number One hit in the U.S. and the U.K., "Honky Tonk Women" is still almost guaranteed to get all the dads dancing at middle-aged parties. It is a great slice of guitar-driven R&B, despite the inevitable embarrassment.

The Creep

Ken Mackintosh and His Orchestra | 1954

A dance craze that swept through Britain—and the U.S. via various cover versions—in the Teddy Boy era of the early '50s, the Creep was banned from many ballrooms because of the "lewd" nature of the close-contact shuffling steps involved. Jeepers, creepers!

The Hustle

Van McCoy | 1975

Despite the numerous one-hit wonder dance crazes that were everywhere throughout the '60s, the Hustle was the first really big dance craze since the Twist. More than any other song, this massive-selling record launched the fashion for disco dancing.

Crazy in Love

Beyoncé | 2003

This big-haired, butt-shakin' onslaught of a track wiped the floor with Beyoncé's previous solo material, storming to the top of the U.S. and U.K. music charts. With the power to instantly fill any dance floor, this track helped the beautiful Ms. Knowles to make the move everyone always knew she was going to make from member of girl group Destiny's Child to center-stage diva in her own right.

Brown Girl in the Ring
Boney M | 1978

Based on a Jamaican nursery rhyme and annoyingly catchy, "Brown Girl in the Ring" was a dance-floor favorite from Euro-disco group Boney M at the height of the '70s disco boom..."tra la la la la."

The Girl from Ipanema
Stan Getz / Astrud Gilberto | 1964

The Brazilian bossa nova craze was sparked by tenor saxophonist Stan Getz and guitarist Charlie Byrd with the 1962 instrumental "Desafinado." The craze peaked two years later with this Getz release—the most famous bossa nova song ever—performed with Brazilian vocalist Astrud Gilberto.

Insomnia
Faithless | 1995

British house music pioneers Sister Bliss and Rollo (brother to the multi-selling chanteuse Dido) were the key players behind this club outfit and "Insomnia" was undoubtedly one of the best moments from their breakthrough year. This is the kind of track that builds a long-term career—and indeed it has!

Mambo Italiano
Rosemary Clooney | 1954

When the mambo dance craze took off in the early '50s, it didn't take long for the Tin Pan Alley tunesmiths to cash in with an abundance of novelty numbers that had little to do with the actual dance. Popular singer and actress Rosemary Clooney gave us one of the best of these novelty tracks, which was later famously re-recorded by Dean Martin.

Love to Love You Baby
Donna Summer | 1975

American disco diva Summer pioneered the Euro-disco sound with German producer Giorgio Moroder on this then-controversial single—Summer's simulated sexual gasps were repeated over insistent synthesized disco beats. The club version ran for 17 minutes, but the shorter cut quickly climbed up the charts in the U.S. and across Europe.

The Wah Watusi
The Orlons | 1962

This one-hit dance wonder by Philadelphia vocal group The Orlons followed in the wake of the worldwide popularity of the Twist. It reached the Number Two spot in the U.S. charts and launched one of the many popular dance crazes that flourished—then swiftly died—in the early '60s.

Groove Is in the Heart
Deee-Lite | 1990

Featuring the bass of Bootsy Collins and the sax of Maceo Parker, this kooky track from the unlikely-looking psychedelic threesome Deee-Lite took New York's dance culture out of the clubs and across the globe. It still manages to get everyone and their grannies up and shaking it on the dance floor 15 years later.

Pull Up to the Bumper
Grace Jones | 1981

Striking-looking Grace Jones was an habitué of New York's ultra-trendy Studio 54 at the height of the disco boom. Her almost androgynous good looks and the musical mix of disco and reggae on this hit single caught the mood of the time perfectly.

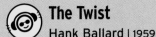 The Twist
Hank Ballard | 1959

Although Chubby Checker popularized this no-hands dance craze, it was as a TV replacement for Hank Ballard—the true originator of the Twist—that Checker got his first big break. If you're looking for the original Twist record (and no doubt someone is), then this Ballard version, released as the flipside to "Teardrops on Your Letter," is it.

Dance, Dance, Dance (Yowsah, Yowsah, Yowsah)
Chic | 1977

Thrusting them to the cutting edge of the disco scene, Chic's debut single established a formula of strong vocals and almost minimalist production, which helped define the dance club music of the era. But the band are probably best-remembered for their 1978 chart topper "Le Freak."

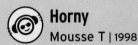 Horny
Mousse T | 1998

An audio overload of brass and hyper-production coupled with the manic refrain of "I'm horny, horny, horny, horny" took this track from the clubs and into the school playground! Mousse T has only come close to such dance perfection once since, with the fun "Is It 'Cos I'm Cool?"

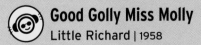 Good Golly Miss Molly
Little Richard | 1958

From the opening bars of Richard's frenetic piano intro that pin your head to the wall, "Good Golly Miss Molly" is a three-minute definition of rock-'n'-roll as dance music. Impossible to stand still to!

Toca's Miracle
Fragma | 2000

Just when people were writing off dance music, here was another track to prove everyone wrong. Blending two previous hits—Fragma's "Toca Me" and Coco's "I Need A Miracle"—paid off even before the start of the summer season that normally spawns such club classics. A hit with critics and clubbers alike.

Limbo Rock
Chubby Checker | 1962

Twist-man Checker tried to recreate his chart-topping success with a few more dance-floor novelties, and this one fared about as well as the rest. But who could forget the limbo? We've all fallen over at some point while bending backwards and trying to dance under a low horizontal bar!

Bang a Gong (Get It On)
T.Rex | 1971

T.Rex's most famous song (released in the U.K. simply as "Get It On") was lightweight as rock-'n'-roll, perhaps, but perfect to get down to. No wonder T.Rex records were chosen for the soundtrack of the hit movie about dance-mad Billy Elliott!

4 My People (Basement Jaxx Remix)
Missy Elliott | 2002

Taken from her highly-acclaimed *Miss E... So Addictive* album, "4 My People" saw rap pioneer Missy Elliott take on a brand new persona as a club diva par excellence. Bringing in Basement Jaxx to remix showed not only how creative she could be, but also how dance could embrace any genre and make it its own.

Free
Ultra Naté | 1997

The only real dance diva of any worth to emerge in the past decade, Baltimore's flamboyant Ultra Naté finally hit the big time with this uplifting power anthem—taken from her third album *Situation: Critical*—that had huge airplay across the U.S. and still refuses to die.

Dancing in the Street
Martha and the Vandellas | 1964

After the 1985 David Bowie and Mick Jagger version, the song became a truly anthemic invitation to dance. Here it is in its first and definitive form from the Motown girl group Martha and the Vandellas—"Are you ready for a brand new beat?"

Livin' La Vida Loca
Ricky Martin | 1999

Riding the crest of the Latino explosion that ended the last century, Ricky Martin introduced the sound to the U.K. for the very first time. The former boy band member and *General Hospital* actor went supernova with this butt-shaking Latino-rock crossover classic.

Call on Me
Eric Prydz | 2004

Steve Winwood's classic "Valerie" was given a makeover by Swedish DJ Prydz in 2004, signaling the start of a series of reworked '80s tunes swamping Europe throughout the following months. "Call on Me" was as famous for its '80s-flavored video featuring attractive spandex-clad women doing aerobics as for hogging the Number One spot in the U.K. for five weeks.

Save the Last Dance for Me
The Drifters | 1960

The most enduring of all dance-floor themes, that of who gets to dance the last dance, was the subject of this classic Drifters hit: "...don't forget who's taking you home, and in whose arms you wanna be." This was the great songwriting team of Leiber and Stoller at their most lyrical.

Boogie Nights
Heatwave | 1977

Another classic hit from the disco era, this time from '70s funk group Heatwave. "Boogie Nights" is the archetype of pop funk aimed firmly at the dance floor—"Dance with the boogie, get down..."

Groovejet
Spiller | 2000

Originally an instrumental that was making good progress on its own merits before Sophie Ellis-Bextor—former frontwoman of indie band theaudience—came on board to propel it to the top of the U.K. charts with her effortless cool. No other track sums up dance island Ibiza quite like it!

Professional Widow (It's Got to Be Big)
Tori Amos | 1997

The bizarre pairing of kooky, spooky singer-songwriter Amos of "Cornflake Girl" fame with the year's big name in dance Armand van Helden proved just how versatile dance music had become—and gave Amos her biggest U.K. hit.

Where's Your Head At?
Basement Jaxx | 2001

Basement Jaxx are cutting-edge British production duo Simon
Ratcliffe and Felix Buxton, and their breakthrough track was this
well-respected progressive house anthem. This is Basement Jaxx
at the height of their powers—critically-acclaimed modern dance
music that it's cool to like.

Walkin' the Dog
Rufus Thomas | 1963

Memphis blues man Rufus Thomas hit the soul market with a series
of novelty dance numbers, including "Do the Funky Chicken," "Do
the Funky Penguin," and his biggest hit, "Walkin' the Dog"—which
was followed, less successfully, by "Can Your Monkey Do the Dog"!

You Make Me Feel (Mighty Real)
Sylvester | 1979

A forerunner of the Hi-NRG movement, this dance anthem featured
a falsetto-voiced Sylvester and a bass line to die for—no wonder it's
been covered by everyone from Ten City's Byron Stingily to
comedienne Sandra Bernhard. A sweat-drenched slice of club
heaven from one of the first openly gay artists to hit the charts.

Theme from S'Express
S'Express | 1988

DJ and producer Mark Moore mixed trendy disco samples from the
likes of '70s soul and disco group Rose Royce with an unforgettable
"I've got the hots for you" hook to hit Number One in the U.K. and
signal the rebirth of the dance era.

Rock Your Baby
George McCrae | 1974

Vintage '70s disco fodder that has stood the test of time, this cheerful song soared to the Number One spot on the American Billboard chart in 1974 before repeating its chart-topping success in countless other countries.

Let's Dance
Chris Montez | 1962

Californian singer Montez enjoyed a brief burst of fame following this dance-floor special, but the catchy record far outlived the fame of its originator. The huge success of "Let's Dance" led to Montez touring the U.K. in 1963, with support from an up-and-coming British group called The Beatles!

Gonna Make You Sweat (Everybody Dance Now)
C&C Music Factory | 1991

With its screeching vocals and fierce metallic hook, this single brought house music to Middle America and club kids to their knees. The product of dance savvy producers Clivillés and Cole, who'd already worked their magic for the likes of Grace Jones and Chaka Khan, this track guaranteed them A-list status.

Tea for Two Cha Cha
Tommy Dorsey and His Orchestra | 1958

A spin-off from the mambo, the cha-cha-cha was a Cuban dance craze that caught on in the U.S. and elsewhere in the late '50s. The biggest cha-cha-cha hits were "Cherry Pink and Apple Blossom White" (written as a mambo by Pérez Prado) and the at-that-time ubiquitous "Tea for Two Cha Cha" by Tommy Dorsey's Orchestra.

The In Crowd
Ramsey Lewis Trio | 1965

Led by soul-funk pianist Lewis, the Trio recorded a clutch of instrumental covers of pop hits, including The Beatles' "A Hard Day's Night" and The McCoys' "Hang on Sloopy." But their first big hit was this live version of a Dobie Gray track, complete with roaring vocals and hand-clapping support from the audience.

Unfinished Sympathy
Massive Attack | 1991

Both innovative and influential, Massive Attack pioneered trip hop—a sound that grew out of Britain's hip-hop and house scenes—and paved the way for the likes of Portishead and Tricky. Nowhere did they do it better than on this atmospheric groove taken from their *Blue Lines* album, which featured vocals by Shara Nelson and was instantly regarded as a classic.

say it with soul

Soul came out of a fusion of the previously exclusive fields of gospel music and the blues. Pioneered by the great Ray Charles and other black musicians, including James Brown and Sam Cooke, in the '50s, soul established itself as *the* pop music of black America throughout the '60s. It has touched almost every other area of popular music since, and there are some wonderful recent examples of today's young singers carrying on the soul tradition in contemporary music. But to get some of the greatest downloads of sacred—as well as secular—soul we have to go back to its roots in black *and* white church music.

I Can See Clearly Now
Ray Charles | 1977

A song of optimism, honed originally by Johnny Nash, but recorded even more memorably and, some would say, ironically in view of his blindness and the song's title by Ray Charles.

Rescue Me
Fontella Bass | 1965

After releasing a couple of duets with blues singer Bobby McClure, soul diva Fontella Bass gave us one of the classic soul hits of the '60s with this self-penned anthem, which was later covered by both Aretha Franklin and Diana Ross.

Superstition
Stevie Wonder | 1972

"Superstition" is one of the great R&B soul records of all time—part synthesized funk, part earthy horn riffs, part polyrhythmic anthem. Sensational, but try dancing to it at your peril!

The Soul Sessions
Joss Stone | 2003

An English rose with a soul-drenched voice that took New York by storm, 16-year-old Joss Stone floored fans and critics alike with her debut album, drawing on such diverse sources as Betty Wright and the White Stripes. Whether she develops into the mature singer everyone is expecting remains to be seen, but to sound on her debut like a time-served practitioner of Black American soul music was nothing short of sensational.

Land of 1000 Dances
Wilson Pickett | 1966

Although he is best known for "In the Midnight Hour," this was Pickett's biggest pop hit and is simply one of the best crowd-stirrers of '60s soul. "Got to know how to pony, like Bony Maronie" –and it's got great lyrics, too!

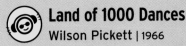

Papa Was a Rollin' Stone
The Temptations | 1972

The Temptations had already moved from a mainstream Motown sound through psychedelic soul when they cut Norman Whitfield and Barrett Strong's "Papa Was a Rollin' Stone"–a brilliant fourth chart topper from one of the all-time great vocal outfits.

In the Midnight Hour
Wilson Pickett | 1965

A true anthem of mid-'60s soul, Pickett's "In the Midnight Hour" was the epitome of the horn and guitar Memphis sound and a dance-floor favorite with Mods everywhere.

End of the Road
Boyz II Men | 1992

Bizarrely, this is the most successful single ever released on Motown. It was the perfect showcase for Boyz II Men's four-part harmonies and it is a heartbreaker of a ballad for anyone who's ever been dumped.

Be Happy
Mary J. Blige | 1994

It's hard to believe that the "Queen of Hip-Hop Soul" was discovered after she recorded a track into a karaoke machine at a mall! Her voice reflects the heartache of her tough background and nowhere does it shine better than on this ghetto classic, produced by Sean "Puffy" Coombs.

Reach Out I'll Be There
The Four Tops | 1966

One of the true anthems of the Motown era and, by far, The Tops' finest moment, this song hit the Number One spot on the American Billboard chart–a feat repeated by the Jackson 5 when they covered it in 1970.

No Woman No Cry
Bob Marley | 1975

Reggae musician Bob Marley is famous for spreading this style of music outside of Jamaica. This track from the album *Live!*, recorded at the London Lyceum, was his breakthrough hit–a melodic infusion of reggae into the popular mainstream.

Live at the Apollo
James Brown | 1963

Following in the footsteps of Ray Charles, James Brown established himself with a frantic live act that usually ended with him literally collapsing at the climax of the show. Recorded in October 1962 at Harlem's Apollo Theater, this was "Soul Brother Number One" at his very best and, according to *Rolling Stone* magazine, this "may be the greatest live album ever recorded."

I've Been Loving You Too Long
Otis Redding | 1965

In the studio, Redding's "I've Been Loving You Too Long" was simply one of the great soul ballad performances. But Otis sweating it out in D. A. Pennebaker's film of the 1967 Monterey Pop Festival completely stole the show from the more "progressive" acts, including Jimi Hendrix and Janis Joplin!

What'd I Say (Parts 1 and 2)
Ray Charles | 1959

From the opening electric piano riff to the closing call-and-response choruses with his backing group the Raelettes, this was a double-sided definition of what soul music was all about it by the man who virtually invented it. "What'd I Say" is one of those rare events—a seminal record that truly changed music forever.

Three Times a Lady
The Commodores | 1978

The Commodores epitomized the "sweet soul" sound on this relaxed romantic ballad. Written by Lionel Richie before he left the group in the early '80s, "Three Times a Lady" topped the charts on both sides of the Atlantic.

On Broadway
The Drifters | 1963

Although the lyrics aren't entirely uncritical—"when you're walking down the street and you ain't had enough to eat"—this song is still one of composers Jerry Leiber and Mike Stoller's greatest paeans to the city of New York.

Shake Your Head

Was (Not Was) | 1992

The ultra-hip Don and David Was (not their real names) scored a nonsensical soul hit with vocals by...wait for it...Ozzy Osbourne and Kim Basinger! Yes, that's the lead singer of Black Sabbath and the actress from *L.A. Confidential*. It's all in the mix by the wonderful dance pioneer Steve "Silk" Hurley.

Baby Love

The Supremes | 1964

The light touch of Diana Ross' voice over the other girls' backing vocals and the super-sharp production made for classic Motown on this single. The Supremes' second U.S. Number One—and only U.K. Number One—"Baby Love" was a benchmark for girl group pop songs thereafter.

Cupid

Johnny Nash | 1970

Texan singer Johnny Nash had a Top 40 hit with this sweet-voiced romantic plea—"Cupid, please hear my cry..."—rivaled only by composer Sam Cooke's original from 1961.

Fingertips (Parts 1 and 2)

Little Stevie Wonder | 1963

The sensational single debut by early Motown protégé "Little" Stevie Wonder, "Fingertips" was a live call-and-response harmonica vehicle that soon had everyone wondering who this chart-topping 12-year-old "Genius" was.

Street Life
The Crusaders featuring Randy Crawford | 1979

Despite featuring on the soundtrack to the entirely forgettable Burt Reynolds movie *Sharky's Machine*, this track is anything but. It also helped establish smooth vocalist Randy Crawford as a soul star in her own right, propelling her to future hits, such as "Almaz" and "One Day I'll Fly Away."

Son of a Preacher Man
Dusty Springfield | 1969

From Dusty Springfield's now-legendary Memphis sessions, "Son of a Preacher Man" was just about the funkiest track Britain's potential—but never quite realized—queen of soul ever cut.

Automatic
The Pointer Sisters | 1984

Sisters Ruth, June, and Anita had come a long way from their days as backup vocalists for disco pioneer Sylvester. Thanks to acclaimed producer Richard Perry, they crafted some of the finest soul records of the '70s and '80s, and this was one of the highlights.

My Girl
The Temptations | 1965

Written by Smokey Robinson and Ronald White of The Miracles, "My Girl" is an absolute gem in the annals of soul ballads, and love songs generally: "I've got sunshine on a cloudy day..."

Georgia on My Mind
Ray Charles | 1960

Although Hoagy Carmichael's original "Georgia on My Mind" had been around since the early '30s, this definitive, emotion-packed version is "...as sweet and clear as moonlight through the pines." It was the first crossover hit for Ray Charles, the man dubbed the high priest of soul.

Young, Gifted, and Black
Bob and Marcia | 1970

A reggae-tinged cover of a Nina Simone song from Jamaican singers Bob Andy and Marcia Griffiths, which was written in the era when "black" was becoming a permissible description of ethnicity for the first time.

Mannish Boy
Muddy Waters | 1955

A one-song definition of an admittedly macho view of what being a man is all about, Muddy Waters' "Mannish Boy" is a classic of country-to-Chicago blues.

Love Is a Hurtin' Thing
Lou Rawls | 1966

With a smooth voice in the Nat King Cole mode, but blessed with an incredible three-octave range, Rawls made some highly effective pop singles that reflected his hugely successful career as a live cabaret artist. His first hit single from his *Soulin'* album, "Love Is a Hurtin' Thing," was seamless blues-edged pop.

I Got You (I Feel Good)
James Brown and The Famous Flames | 1966

A landmark in '60s soul by the self-titled "Godfather of Soul," this has been revived several times and is still Brown's best-known song—now considered a true classic.

Can't Get Enough of Your Love, Babe
Barry White | 1974

One of several hits from the king of soul kitsch—though he is rarely acknowledged as such. Fans of the heavy-breathing lover-man take him far too seriously for that!

I Say a Little Prayer
Aretha Franklin | 1968

Surely one of the ultimate soul records: Lady Soul exercises that gospel-trained voice of gold on this clever Burt Bacharach classic of longing: "The moment I wake up, before I put on my make-up..." While the song's been covered many times over the years, no one sings it quite like Aretha.

Blue Light 'Til Dawn
Cassandra Wilson | 1993

Not afraid to take chances, Cassandra Wilson—with her distinctive and flexible voice—experimented with free funk and straight standards before finding herself artistically with this riveting acoustic blues-oriented album. It set the course for her highly individual style from thereon.

Back to Life (However Do You Want Me)
Soul II Soul | 1989

U.K. soul? Yes, and for once it wasn't just a poor relation to its U.S. counterparts! Producer Jazzie B was truly groundbreaking on this anthemic track, which hit it big on both sides of the Atlantic. A powerful mix of soul, reggae, and hip-hop beats, with vocals from Caron Wheeler, that truly defined a moment in the late '80s.

Knock on Wood
Eddie Floyd | 1966

Eddie Floyd's biggest hit was one of the defining tracks of the Memphis soul sound and it became a mainstay in any playlist of '60s soul groups with club DJs everywhere.

Tired of Being Alone
Al Green | 1971

Soul-man Al Green fitted this description literally when, after a string of hits, including this million-seller, he became a preacher and began conducting services from the Full Gospel Tabernacle church in Memphis.

Down Home Girl
Alvin Robinson | 1964

With a descending horn riff and laidback delivery, "Down Home Girl" is a gem of New Orleans '60s soul—albeit one recorded in New York City. Produced by songwriters Leiber and Stoller, this is a left-handed compliment—"Lord I swear the perfume you wear, was made out of turnip greens"—to a real country chick.

Playing for Keeps
Darlene Love | 1963

This was the riveting flipside to "(Today I Met) The Boy I'm Gonna Marry" from producer Phil Spector's protégée Darlene Love, who charted briefly in the early '60s before turning to acting in the '80s.

Lovin' You
Minnie Riperton | 1979

Soul singer Riperton's five-octave range handled this delicate, ethereal song with a controlled restraint that enchanted listeners. The birds singing in the background just added to the magic.

My Guy
Mary Wells | 1964

Sweet-voiced Mary Wells was one of the first Motown stars to enjoy a string of hits—all written for her by Smokey Robinson—with tight, confident backing arrangements that set the style for the label's trademark sound. Faultless.

Ray Charles at Newport
Ray Charles | 1958

When Ray Charles, already a hero of black America, ripped things apart at the Newport Jazz Festival in 1958, the broader jazz audience picked up their ears. Between instrumentals, Ray stunned the crowds with "I Got a Woman," a searing "Drown in My Own Tears," and "Night Time Is the Right Time"—where he was almost blown off stage himself by the erotically-charged vocal interventions of Margie Hendricks.

Church
Lyle Lovett | 1992

From his album *Joshua Judges Ruth*, "Church" is a hand-clapping congregational evocation of a down-home Southern church meeting. The story concerns a longer-than-usual sermon delivered while everyone's waiting to get back home to eat dinner. Inspirational nevertheless.

Twist and Shout
The Isley Brothers | 1962

A soul music institution in their own right, The Isley Brothers' most financially successful songs were "Shout" and its follow-up—cashing in on the Twist dance craze—"Twist and Shout" when they were covered by Lulu and The Beatles, respectively.

Sneakin' Sally through the Alley
Robert Palmer | 1974

Classic white soul on a song taken from Robert Palmer's album of the same name, written by New Orleans veteran Allen Toussaint, and performed with The Meters from that same city, where it was also recorded.

Memphis Soul Stew
King Curtis | 1967

Fluid tenor sax player Curtis was recognizable—though anonymous—as the session soloist on scores of R&B and pop hits by the likes of Nat King Cole, Joe Turner, LaVern Baker, Bobby Darin, Sam Cooke, The Drifters, and, most famously, The Coasters. Records under his own name didn't do so well, with the classic single "Memphis Soul Stew" being one of only two to make the charts.

When a Man Loves a Woman
Percy Sledge | 1966

This was an auspicious debut from Percy Sledge, whose majestic voice contributed to one of *the* romantic soul anthems of the mid '60s.

Forget Me Nots
Patrice Rushen | 1982

A jazz pianist with a light vocal style, Patrice released a series of spectacularly different, classy soul albums on Elektra Records. "Forget Me Nots" was her biggest hit and it's since been sampled on tracks by Will Smith, George Michael, and several others.

I've Got News for You
Ray Charles | 1961

Featuring the cream of the Count Basie orchestra, Ray Charles delivered the ultimate big band blues on his album *Genius + Soul = Jazz*. With humorous lyrics and a take-no-prisoners organ solo, the impact of this track is consistently mind-boggling.

Ladies' Night
Kool and the Gang | 1979

Starting out as a jazz ensemble in the '60s, then becoming a funk band in the '70s, Kool and the Gang morphed into an R&B outfit with the popular track "Ladies' Night." They recruited the sensational James Taylor as lead vocalist to pack a punch on this classy hit, which, sadly, has since been downgraded to a bachelorette party theme tune.

Pick Up the Pieces
Average White Band | 1975

From Scotland, the Average White Band specialized in soul-funk of a very North American flavor. At the sharp end technically, their crisp style and immaculate arrangements were epitomized on their biggest hit, the U.S. chart topper "Pick Up the Pieces" from their best-selling *AWB* album.

(I'm a) Road Runner
Junior Walker and the All Stars | 1966

The nearest thing to raw R&B to appear on the smooth-soul-dominated Motown label, sax-man Walker wailed his way through some raucous instrumentals including this '60s dance floor smash.

I Heard It through the Grapevine
Marvin Gaye | 1968

"I Heard It through the Grapevine" was Marvin Gaye's first chart topper in America and it became his best-remembered number, beloved of soul performers ever after.

I Never Loved a Man (The Way I Love You) / Do Right Woman, Do Right Man
Aretha Franklin | 1967

The epitome of her style of spine-tingling southern soul, this was a double-sided sensation when it was released just after Aretha moved to Atlantic Records and began working with new producers. Goose bumps guaranteed!

Family Affair
Sly and the Family Stone | 1971

Heralding the disco and funk styles of the coming decade, Stone's records of the late '60s and early '70s constituted the cutting edge of black American music at that time. The hit single "Family Affair" and the album *There's a Riot Goin' On* marked a move to a more political stance from the goodtime psychedelia of their earlier hits.

Don't Let It Get You Down
The Crusaders | 1973

Jazz-funk pioneers The Crusaders led the crossover trend in the '70s with a style that one critic described as "soulful Muzak."

I Love Your Smile
Shanice | 1991

This was a massive summery hit for Motown by a gal who'd been singing on commercials since she was only eight years old. Capturing the real joie-de-vivre of being a teen, "I Love Your Smile" is perky and cute, and if you can track down the Ben Liebrand remix, you'll be smiling too.

JUKEBOX
FAVORITES

From the moment the first nickel was dropped into a magical, musical box through to its '50s and '60s heyday, the jukebox thrived in bars, diners, dance clubs, and the like, bringing the best rock-'n'-roll and pop hits to eager teenage ears. What stayed on a jukebox, or nickelodeon, for any length of time—in other words, what the kids would pay hard cash to hear rather than just listen to for free over the radio—was once considered as valid a sign of a record's popularity as the sales charts. Jukebox records were the backbone of the music industry, with many a classic never topping the charts, but gaining huge popularity all the same. Their popularity may have waned, but jukes are still out there and some of today's songs would be absolute naturals if the boxes were to make a big digital-era comeback.

See You Later, Alligator
Bobby Charles | 1955

A huge hit for Bill Haley in 1956, this song's writer Bobby Charles released a much jumpier original before Haley's cover in the R&B style of his native New Orleans.

In the Summertime
Mungo Jerry | 1970

A skiffly goodtime disc that cheered the summer months of 1970 "...when the weather is high" and has endured ever since—which is more than can be said for four-piece pub group Mungo Jerry.

The Stripper
David Rose | 1962

From the moment composer David Rose hit the charts with his instrumental "The Stripper," the soundtrack to all future strip shows was set in concrete. You simply couldn't—indeed can't—think of a stripper doing her thing without this burlesque-flavored tune being conjured up in your mind.

Chantilly Lace
The Big Bopper | 1958

DJ Jiles Perry Richardson Jr., aka the Big Bopper, was a larger-than-life character whose brief, but successful, career in the musical limelight came to a tragic end in the same plane crash that killed Buddy Holly and Ritchie Valens. This classic jukebox hit still brings a smile..."Hellooo Baby!"

Tequila
The Champs | 1958

This frantic, catchy Latin-influenced instrumental about a Mexican liquor was a one-off hit for L.A. session men the Champs. Needless to say, their follow-ups "El Rancho Rock" and "Too Much Tequila" failed to cash in on its success.

Only in America
Jay and the Americans | 1963

Originally written for the Drifters by Leiber and Stoller, Barry Mann, and Cynthia Weil, "Only in America" was a Latin-tinged song of optimistic patriotism released by Jay and his aptly-named group.

Whole Lotta Shakin' Goin' On
Jerry Lee Lewis | 1957

Along with "Great Balls of Fire," which it preceded, this is the definitive example of the fiery boogie and wild vocals that made Jerry Lee—and his Pumping Piano—a star.

Rock 'n' Roll
John Lennon | 1975

John Lennon's celebration of his rock-'n'-roll roots was an amazing collection of covers of classic records, including Gene Vincent's "Be-Bop-A-Lula," Ben E. King's "Stand By Me," Chuck Berry's "Sweet Little Sixteen," Buddy Holly's "Peggy Sue," and other unforgettable rock songs in the same vein.

La Bamba
Ritchie Valens | 1959

Released as the flipside to the record "Donna," this contagious piece of Latino rock was inspired by a traditional Mexican folk song. Recorded when Valens was just 17 years old, this popular rock-'n'-roll song has stood the test of time—"Arriba, arriba!"

Wipe Out
The Surfaris | 1963

Simple but atmospheric, this hit was the B-side to "Surfer Joe" and it was one of the few surf music instrumentals.

Reet Petite
Jackie Wilson | 1957

This R&B pop classic, written by Berry Gordy, Jr. just before he set up Motown Records, combined Wilson's athletic voice with a roaring big band to produce a record that would leave you breathless.

Hotel California
The Eagles | 1977

Soft rock's not a term you hear much any more, but at the time The Eagles' effortless harmonies and easy-on-the ear country epitomized the genre. This track from their critically acclaimed album of the same name remains a firm favorite with fans and would, no doubt, be a popular choice on any modern jukebox.

Israelites
Desmond Dekker | 1968

Still familiar decades after it was first released, this reggae smash is the most memorable of a string of hits Dekker enjoyed in the late '60s. It hit the Number One spot in the U.K. and was also the first Jamaican song ever to make it into the Top Ten on the U.S. charts.

Slow Down
Larry Williams | 1958

If I had just one choice of any vintage rock-'n'-roll record to play on a jukebox, this would be it. Rough at the edges, solid at the center. Unbeatable!

Ruby Baby
Dion | 1963

After he broke with his backing group the Belmonts, Brooklyn-born Dion DiMucci went on to make a clutch of tough-sounding R&B tracks, including this searing version of an early Drifters hit.

Music! Music! Music!
Teresa Brewer | 1950

Dedicated to that 20th-century musical phenomenon, the jukebox—or, as it is called in the song, the nickelodeon—"Music! Music! Music!" was a jukebox favorite in 1950 and it became Brewer's signature song.

Book of Love
The Monotones | 1958

New Jersey doo-woppers The Monotones had just one hit. This literary love ditty made it to Number Five on the U.S. Billboard chart and was clearly aimed at the teenage market: "Chapter one says you love her, you love her with all your heart..."

You Can't Judge a Book by the Cover
Bo Diddley | 1962

"I look like a farmer, but I'm a lover" sang Diddley on this slice of cool philosophy written by Willie Dixon. One of the Chicago R&B star's biggest records, this was also a favorite with the young white bands he helped inspire.

Raunchy
Bill Justis | 1957

Riff-based bluesy sax number "Raunchy" was one of the earliest rock-'n'-roll instrumentals, heralding a minor trend for pop-oriented instrumentals by the likes of Duane Eddy.

Danny's All-Star Joint
Rickie Lee Jones | 1979

On this track from her commercially and critically acclaimed debut album simply named *Rickie Lee Jones*, cool, cool Rickie jive talks her way downstairs at Danny's, where "They got a juke box that goes doyt-doyt."

Shake, Rattle and Roll
Joe Turner | 1954

Before Bill Haley cleaned up the lyrics somewhat—helping to launch rock-'n'-roll in the process—blues shouter Joe Turner laid down the original version of this song as a strident piece of no-nonsense, sexually explicit R&B.

I Know (You Don't Love Me No More)
Barbara George | 1962

R&B singer and songwriter Barbara George's exclamatory style was perfectly suited to this defiant song of resignation.

Stay
Maurice Williams and the Zodiacs | 1960

Later covered by The Four Seasons, The Hollies, Jackson Browne, and Cyndi Lauper, this chart-topping classic rendition—known by many today because it was included on the *Dirty Dancing* soundtrack—was never really equaled for raw, soaring power.

Just a Gigolo / I Ain't Got Nobody
Louis Prima and Keely Smith | 1958

Italian-American Louis Prima made several celebrated jump-band duets with his musical partner and wife Keely Smith, including this wonderful, effortless segue from "Gigolo" to "Nobody" in a live Las Vegas performance.

Not Fade Away
The Rolling Stones | 1964

In retrospect, a Buddy Holly cover seems a surprising record to be the Stones' first U.K. Top Ten entry, but with its Bo Diddley style beat, "Not Fade Away" gelled perfectly with the British R&B style the group represented at the time.

Bony Moronie
Larry Williams | 1957

Solid '50s rock-'n'-roll, this song was in the same mold lyrically as Little Richard's "Long Tall Sally"—as was Williams' other hit "Short Fat Fanny." Williams gave these songs his own distinct style by whistling what would otherwise have been the sax part.

Last Night
Mar-Keys | 1961

Stax Records session men Steve Cropper, "Duck" Dunn, and the rest of the band, who later formed the basis of Booker T. and the MGs, had their biggest hit with this funky instrumental beloved of soul bands of the time.

Hound Dog
Willie Mae "Big Mama" Thornton | 1953

The wild original of "Hound Dog," crafted by Leiber and Stoller and performed by blues singer "Big Mama" went to Number One on the U.S. R&B chart three years before Elvis' huge hit version emerged.

Ain't Got No Home
Clarence "Frogman" Henry | 1956

The "Frogman" earned his nickname with his imitations of ol' croaky on this debut piece of New Orleans hokum: "I can sing like a girl and I can sing like a frog."

The Nitty Gritty
Shirley Ellis | 1963

Equally remembered for her two nursery-rhyme style songs "The Name Game" and "The Clapping Song," Shirley Ellis started her funky, but brief, sojourn in the pop charts with this contribution to the hip vocabulary.

Lawdy Miss Clawdy
Lloyd Price | 1952

"Lawdy Miss Clawdy" was an early R&B hit from Louisiana singer Price, which was covered many times in later years, not least by Elvis Presley as the flipside to "Shake Rattle and Roll" in 1956.

The Train Kept A-Rollin'
Johnny Burnette and the Rock-'n'-Roll Trio | 1956

With his brother Dorsey and guitarist Paul Burlison, singer Johnny Burnette formed the Rock-'n'-Roll Trio in 1955, only to be rejected by Sun Records because they sounded too much like Elvis! Their brief career together still produced some gems of pure rockabilly.

Rocking Goose
Johnny and the Hurricanes | 1960

With an insistent "goose squawk" honked by leader Johnny Paris on his saxophone, this somewhat annoying record was, nevertheless, a massive hit and it was typical of the many novelty instrumentals of the period.

Way Down Yonder in New Orleans
Freddy Cannon | 1959

Sandpaper-voiced Cannon enjoyed a clutch of raucous, horn-backed hits typified by this over-the-top update of an old jazz song from the '20s.

Drunk
Jimmy Liggins | 1953

Fun, up-tempo rhythm and booze from R&B man Jimmy Liggins on this novelty celebration of inebriation released on the highly influential Specialty Records label.

Quarter to Three
Gary "U.S." Bonds | 1960

Bonds' raucous but infectious sound on "the swingin'est song that could ever be" was typical of several hit records in the early '60s, with the almost homemade-sounding use of tape echo and phasing giving "Quarter to Three" its trademark fuzzy effect.

Little Darlin'

The Diamonds | 1957

Memorable among doo-wop hits, if only for its sheer production values, The Diamonds' version of "Little Darlin'" had an over-the-top arrangement that used every vocal group trick in the book. Like most of the all-white group's hits, this was copied from an original by a black group—in this case, The Gladiolas.

Rudy's Rock

Bill Haley and His Comets | 1956

Musically one of the best records Haley and His Comets ever made, "Rudy's Rock" was one of the first rock-'n'-roll instrumentals featuring the great tenor sax man Rudy Pompilli.

Lights Out

Jerry Byrne | 1958

Mac "Dr. John" Rebennack co-wrote this frantic rocker for Byrne from the Specialty Records school of New Orleans rock-'n'-roll.

She's about a Mover
Sir Douglas Quintet | 1965

Described by one writer as "a blend of Texas pop and The Beatles' "She's a Woman"," this energetic helping of Tex-Mex rock-'n'-roll made for an irresistible hit.

Rebel Rouser
Duane Eddy | 1958

A "twangy" guitar sound—with the melody played on the bass strings—was the echo-drenched trademark on all of Duane Eddy's heavily amplified hits, including this breakthrough record that made it into the American Top Ten.

Take it Easy, Greasy
Bobby Charles | 1956

R&B singer and songwriter Bobby Charles, who is best remembered for "See You Later, Alligator," performed on this track in his traditional New Orleans shuffle-beat mode.

Wichita Lineman
Glen Campbell | 1968

Jimmy Webb exploited the romance in various place names of the American West in a bunch of hits he wrote for Glen Campbell, including "By the Time I Get to Phoenix," "Galveston," and this hit, which made it to Number Three on the U.S. singles chart.

Respect
Aretha Franklin | 1967

Originally written by Otis Redding, "Respect" became one of *the* clarion calls of '60s black America with this version by top soul vocalist Aretha Franklin, backed with a blues riff that confirmed her status as "Soul Sister Number One."

Monster Mash
Bobby Pickett and the Crypt Kickers | 1962

Jumping on the back of the early '60s dance craze obsession, Pickett's dirge-like narrative and Boris Karloff impressions made for an incredibly popular novelty song that was also a great rock-'n'-roll record. A perennial Halloween favorite, it hit the charts again in 1973—"It was a graveyard smash."

Rock around the Clock
Bill Haley and His Comets | 1954

Twelve months before Elvis released "Heartbreak Hotel," balding Bill Haley had already launched rock-'n'-roll with this single, the genre's first great anthem. It initially featured in the juvenile-delinquent film drama *Blackboard Jungle*, followed by the first rock movie *Rock Around the Clock*, which sparked riots in cinemas worldwide. Nothing was the same again.

LOVE & TEARS

It goes without saying that the overwhelming majority of popular songs have been love songs of one kind or another. Among them there have been a core of classic romantic songs that are simply ageless in their poetry and universal appeal. But love stories do not always end happily. Many of the great romances have been about heartache and tragedy. A good sob story is a fairly reliable bet for record companies, and a classic tearjerker can lead musicians, songwriters, and producers crying all the way to the bank. The power of the right words perfectly combined with the right music to evoke an emotional response is undeniable. Every decade has produced its share of memorable, inspirational love songs and poignant tearjerkers that flood us with powerful emotions and memories from the very first note, and here is just a selection of them.

The Tracks of My Tears
Smokey Robinson and the Miracles | 1968

Sweet-voiced Smokey and the Miracles were an essential ingredient in the Motown mix throughout the '70s, Smokey being the right-hand man to label boss Berry Gordy. As pop songs go, "The Tracks of My Tears" counts among the most magnificent and it really does it in the wringing-out-of-every-last-emotion stakes.

Layla
Derek and the Dominos | 1970

"Layla" was Eric Clapton's dedication to his wife-to-be Patti Boyd, who was still married to his friend George Harrison when he wrote this. It was an instant hit and a rock classic—people even named their kids Layla after this song!

Every Time We Say Goodbye
Ella Fitzgerald | 1956

This was the ultimate in "farewell" love songs from the beautiful voice of jazz legend Ella Fitzgerald and the poignant pen of songwriter Cole Porter.

I Can't Make You Love Me
Bonnie Raitt | 1991

Covered by George Michael, Prince, and even Patti Labelle, this version of one of the saddest songs of unrequited love ever written wrings every last tear from the situation as a woman realizes there's nothing she can do to have her love returned: "I can't make your heart feel something it won't." Heartbreaking.

Hero
Enrique Iglesias | 2001

Despite the success of his Ricky Martin-like single "Bailamos,"
Enrique was simply seen as the son of Spanish crooner Julio
Iglesias and boyfriend of tennis star Anna Kournikova. "Hero"
changed all that. A real punch-the-air ballad that appealed to both
men and women alike, this single briefly made Iglesias Jr. the
hottest property in pop.

Lean on Me
Bill Withers | 1972

One of the great romantic songs of the '70s, singer-songwriter Bill
Withers' warm delivery perfectly matched the gentle touch of the
lyrics: "I'll be your friend, I'll help you carry on."

My Funny Valentine
Frank Sinatra | 1953

This love song came from Sinatra's 1954 "comeback" album *Songs
for Young Lovers*, released after his musical career had been on a
serious downturn. Interpretations of Rodgers and Hart classics
simply don't get any better than this.

Beautiful Boy
John Lennon | 1980

"Life is just what happens to you while you're busy making other
plans..." sang Lennon so memorably on this the most lyrical track
from his final album, *Double Fantasy*, which was released just before
his tragic death. The "beautiful boy" of the title was his five-year-
old son, Sean.

Stand by Me
Ben E. King | 1960

Based on a 1955 gospel song of the same name by The Staple Singers, Ben E. King recorded this shortly after leaving The Drifters in 1960 and immediately established his reputation as a solo artist.

True Love
Bing Crosby and Grace Kelly | 1956

"Love forever true" from the film *High Society*, this romantic duet written by the great lyricist Cole Porter has become far more indelible in the popular consciousness than the movie itself.

Get Here
Oleta Adams | 1990

Proving particularly meaningful for troops and their loved ones during the first Gulf War, this version of Brenda Russell's poignant song of absence and longing became a huge hit—and has since become a favorite with *Pop Idol* wannabes.

Me and Bobby McGee
Kris Kristofferson | 1971

Later covered by Johnny Cash and Janis Joplin among others, this classic bittersweet love song came from the pen of country singer-songwriter Kristofferson: "Freedom's just another word for nothin' left to lose."

The Green, Green Grass of Home
Tom Jones | 1966

The Welshman's big voice was never more at home than on this powerful and chart-topping version of Porter Waggoner's emotive song about a condemned prisoner on death row.

With a Song in My Heart
Ella Fitzgerald | 1956

The soaring melody of this Rodgers and Hart classic was written in 1930 and then covered by many fine vocalists before Ella—as with so many songs—made it her own.

Ginny Come Lately
Brian Hyland | 1962

One of the many lightweight singers that characterized U.S. pop in the years before the British invasion, Hyland nevertheless came up with one of the most evocative love songs of the era.

Endless Love
Diana Ross and Lionel Richie | 1981

This über ballad brought two Motown legends together to produce an ever-popular love song that way outlived the movie it came from. It has since been covered by Mariah Carey and Luther Vandross, but the original is still the best. Both at the peak of their powers, Ross and Richie would arguably never be as good again.

Walk on By
Dionne Warwick | 1964

Forever associated with the songs of Burt Bacharach, Warwick's hits by the great composer included "Anyone Who Had a Heart" and "I Say a Little Prayer," as well as the hauntingly lonely classic "Walk on By."

Cry Me a River
Julie London | 1957

One of the highlights of the otherwise rock-'n'-roll-dominated movie *The Girl Can't Help It* was the image of a slinkily-dressed Julie London emotionally singing her sultry version of this class ballad.

You've Got a Friend
Carole King | 1971

One of the great modern love songs, Carole King's masterpiece "You've Got a Friend" from her *Tapestry* album was a palliative to broken hearts everywhere.

Time after Time
Cyndi Lauper | 1984

Originally thought of as a sort of Madonna wannabe with a wacky line in fluorescent hair, ratty clothes, and gimmicky pop songs like "Girls Just Wanna Have Fun," this classy track took Lauper to a whole new level, bringing her the sort of credibility that has lasted to this day.

I Almost Lost My Mind
Pat Boone | 1956

Despite his cleaner-than-clean image, '50s crooner Pat Boone took
a stab at various rock-'n'-roll and R&B numbers with varying
degrees of success. His take of frantic rockers like "Long Tall Sally"
was often embarrassing, but he made a more convincing job of
blues-based ballads like this one, originally by Ivory Joe Hunter.

My Coloring Book
Dusty Springfield | 1963

The sob in British soul singer Dusty Springfield's voice made this
the perfect rendition of a true song of heartbreak.

I Drove All Night
Roy Orbison | 1992

No stranger to a dramatic love song, Roy Orbison brought an
emotional depth to this ballad about just taking off to be with the
one you love, which was released after his death. Drive time has
never packed such a punch.

Love and Affection
Joan Armatrading | 1976

Since singer-songwriter Tracy Chapman made this genre her own,
Joan Armatrading's voice and style haven't seemed quite as unique
as they did when she brought out this classic in the '70s. So slow
it sometimes almost stops, but with the most brilliantly inventive
structure, "Love and Affection" sounds modern even today.

I Remember You
Chet Baker | 1955

This is not the 1962 yodeling abomination by Frank Ifield, but a cooler-than-cool vocal of the great Johnny Mercer composition by trumpeter, and one of the few jazz pinups, Chet Baker.

I'm Not in Love
10cc | 1975

A famous statement of denial—"It's just a silly phase I'm going through"—in one of the most evocative love songs of the '70s. Painstakingly produced with layer upon layer of overdubs, this was a great record too.

I'd Rather Go Blind
Etta James | 1968

With a raw lyric destined to hit you where it hurts, blues star Etta reveals she'd rather lose her sight than watch her lover walk away. This heartrending song became a lethal weapon in the hands of one of the most underrated voices of her time.

Nothing Compares 2 U
Sinead O'Connor | 1990

With a minimalist arrangement, impassioned vocals, and a stunning video in which Sinead cries beautifully to a camera that never moves, this Prince-penned song conquered the world. The fact that Sinead has never done anything else to even touch it proves that sometimes it's about the song more than the singer.

Let's Stay Together
Al Green | 1971

"Let's Stay Together" was later covered by Tina Turner, Shirley Bassey, and many others, but nowhere does it sound as good as on the parping, brassy original by Reverend Al Green—recorded before he took orders, when he was still wearing leather pants. As sexy as it is romantic, this is a classic by anyone's standards.

Unforgettable
Nat King Cole | 1961

A perfect example of pure cocktail lounge romance of the mellow kind from smoky-voiced Nat King Cole.

Against All Odds
Phil Collins | 1984

Phil Collins wrote this bittersweet love song for a forgettable '80s thriller set in the world of pro football—yes, there really was a film about this! It has since been resurrected in Canada, Europe, and the U.K. as a collaboration between American diva Mariah Carey and Irish boy band Westlife.

Songs for Swingin' Lovers
Frank Sinatra | 1956

This album was the ultimate declaration of Sinatra as a swinger. Flawlessly arranged by Nelson Riddle, this bunch of finger-clicking classics came to define up-tempo balladeering from then on in. Simply magical.

If You Go Away
Dusty Springfield | 1967

This fine English version of a tearjerker by the French-speaking Belgian composer Jacques Brel is another example of the talented Ms. Springfield tugging at our heartstrings.

Every Breath You Take
The Police | 1983

The Police's clever, though somewhat knowing, jazz and reggae-influenced style was enormously successful, but sometimes lacked the melodic edge and emotional incisiveness of this hit song of jealousy—the strongest number in their book.

Sylvia's Mother
Dr. Hook and the Medicine Show | 1972

This was written by composer and cartoonist Shel Silverstein as a send-up of country weepers, but record buyers took the lyrics—of the lovelorn caller speaking to his ex's mother on the phone—seriously, and made "Sylvia's Mother" a mammoth hit.

You're Still the One
Shania Twain | 1998

Before the glitz and comedy of her later, more successful tracks "That Don't Impress Me Much" and "Man! I Feel Like a Woman," Canadian singer-songwriter Twain was coming up with beautiful modern country tracks, and none more heartrending than this. "You're Still the One" was the song that took her from respected country singer to best-selling pop superstar.

You Are My Sunshine
Bryan Ferry | 1974

This is one of the songs my mother sang to me—in fact, it's the first song I remember ever hearing. Originally a hit for Gene Autry in the '40s, Ray Charles also recorded a raunchy R&B version in the '60s, but my favorite has to be Bryan Ferry's bluesy '70s tearjerker.

D-I-V-O-R-C-E
Tammy Wynette | 1968

Country singer Tammy's hand-on-the-heart statements about the trials of womanhood, like "Stand by Your Man," seemed out of place with contemporary attitudes, but still struck a chord with millions of listeners. As overtly sentimental schmaltz, this track sure takes some beating.

Memories Are Made of This
Dean Martin | 1956

Dino's casual charm, worn-in good looks, and smooth voice couldn't go wrong on laidback love songs like this.

The Pain of Loving You
Dolly Parton, Linda Ronstadt, Emmylou Harris | 1987

Sounding like a choir of angels, the three women once dubbed the "Three Tenors" of country music, opened their *Trio* album with a moving performance of a Dolly Parton song addressing the hurt that can occur in relationships.

The Winner Takes It All
Abba | 1980

As the Swedish super-group neared the end of their career, the tensions in their romantic relationships really started to come to the surface, though "Knowing Me, Knowing You" gave us an inkling years before. With all the perfect pop sounds we'd come to expect from Abba, this song still had melancholy seeping through every line.

Help Me Make It through the Night
John Holt | 1974

An up-tempo reggae version of a Kris Kristofferson classic from the album *1000 Volts of Holt*, this was written for lonely lovers everywhere—"Tonight I need a friend."

The Folks Who Live on the Hill
Peggy Lee | 1957

A wonderfully evocative paean to growing old gracefully from the pen of Jerome Kern with a tear-jerking arrangement conducted by Frank Sinatra. Simply the best.

Unchained Melody
The Righteous Brothers | 1965

Perhaps the most over-recorded song in pop history, this is best known as a Righteous Brothers' track—or perhaps as that song played during the pottery wheel scene in the movie *Ghost*! It has infiltrated every part of the pop consciousness. Even the legendary Joni Mitchell, not known for her covers, used parts of the song in "Chinese Café."

You're My Best Friend
Don Williams | 1975

A deep-voiced country singer with a laidback style, Don Williams was at his most appealingly intimate with this gentle tearjerker.

I Will Always Love You
Dolly Parton | 1974

Transformed into one of the biggest-selling singles of its decade by Whitney Houston in 1992 when it was included in the hit movie *The Bodyguard*, this love song probably still works best in the hands of its writer, Dolly Parton. She treats it very gently and without any of the vocal fireworks of Whitney's later version.

Frank Sinatra Sings for Only the Lonely
Frank Sinatra | 1958

Sinatra wrings every ounce of emotion out of the lyrics, but with utter taste and economy, on this collection of melancholy love songs, considered by many as his finest achievement. "Willow Weep for Me," "Blues in the Night," and "Ebb Tide" are all masterpieces—not to mention the ultimate version of "One for My Baby (and One More for the Road)."

TEENAGE ★ KICKS

Since the advent of rock-'n'-roll, pop music has
produced its quota of teenage kicks—malcontent
music that puts a finger up at the adult world
and all it stands for. Mod and metal, punk and
grunge, hip-hop and gangsta rap—all have been
used to say a musical "up yours" by disaffected
youth. Much to the alarm of exasperated parents,
preachers, and teachers, who have seen this music
as nothing less than a harbinger of adolescent
anarchy! And if the kids aren't revolting, they still
have more than their share of doom and gloom. In
every generation, there have been plenty of
musicians willing to write enough teen traumas, broken
hearts, and angst-ridden anthems—just think songs of
elopement, high school crushes, "death discs," Public
Enemy, The Smiths, or almost anything by The Shangri-Las—
to satisfy even the most moody adolescent. Perhaps those
parents that were teenagers in the '50s, '60s, and '70s have
got a lot more in common with their hostile, sulky offspring
than they realize.

Subterranean Homesick Blues
Bob Dylan | 1965

The enduring image of this stream-of-consciousness clarion call to disaffected youth was from its promotional clip—a precursor to the pop video—shot in a London back alley. In the video, a mute Dylan faced the camera and flipped through a series of flash cards showing key words from the song, as his friend, the poet Allen Ginsberg, hovered in the background.

A Teenager in Love
Dion and the Belmonts | 1959

An exercise in adolescent self-pity, this doo-wop hit spoke to teenagers everywhere. Cole Porter romance it ain't, but it's certainly late '50s teen trauma through and through.

Another Brick in the Wall
Pink Floyd | 1979

The chorus of schoolchildren chanting at the beginning of Pink Floyd's biggest hit single set the mood perfectly for this bleak song of a desolate future: "We don't need no education, we don't need no thought control..."

Nevermind
Nirvana | 1991

A crucial album in '90s rock, *Nevermind* was a seminal release from the pioneers of the indie-driven grunge movement and it shot Kurt Cobain, David Grohl, and Kris Novoselic to superstardom. The album includes their best-known single "Smells Like Teen Spirit," which became an instant teen anthem.

Leader of the Pack
The Shangri-Las | 1964

"Death discs" had a special place in teen-oriented music of the
'50s and '60s, and this ever-popular dramatic hit with its roaring
motorcycle and crashing glass sound effects was quite simply the
most celebrated of them all. The leader of the pack, no less.

Yakety Yak
The Coasters | 1958

The Coasters identified with put-upon kids everywhere in this
Leiber and Stoller classic, which became their most enduring hit–
"Don't talk back!"

At Seventeen
Janis Ian | 1975

Having written her first controversial hit "Society's Child" at the
age of 14, Ian was already an established singer-songwriter when
she won a Grammy for her teen angst ballad "At Seventeen," which
so many adolescent girls immediately identified with.

I Get Around
The Beach Boys | 1964

Sun-'n'-sea-'n'-sand–and lots of girls of course–together with the
boys' trademark vocal harmonies made this their first American
Number One and a perennially popular choice for hip teenagers
cruisin' around in their cars. This was the West Coast surfing sound
at its classiest.

Why Do Fools Fall in Love?
Frankie Lymon and the Teenagers | 1956

Street-corner doo-woppers Frankie Lymon and the Teenagers arguably made it too big, too young. Lymon was only 13 when they cut this record and his career ended with drug abuse and his early death in the mid '60s. But this still-played smash hit was *the* teenybop anthem of its day.

Bang Bang (My Baby Shot Me Down)
Cher | 1966

Written by her husband Sonny Bono, Cher's doom-laden opus struck a chord with desperate—but perhaps not *that* desperate—lovers everywhere. Nancy Sinatra's cover version also recently enjoyed a revival after Quentin Tarantino chose it as the theme to his movie *Kill Bill*.

Ruby Tuesday
Melanie | 1970

Flower child Melanie had her biggest hit with "Brand New Key" in 1971, but this cover of the Rolling Stones' hit released the year before showed her often fragile delivery at its most effective.

Sweet Little Sixteen
Chuck Berry | 1958

I can remember precisely when I first heard this evocation of an archetypal American teenage girl on a Wurlitzer jukebox in a penny arcade in the small coastal town where I grew up—and she still sounds just as young today.

The Clash
The Clash | 1977

Part of the first wave of British punk, The Clash delivered the kind of politically charged anger on record that most of their spiky-haired contemporaries just spouted in interviews. They released separate U.K. and U.S. versions of their debut album with different songs on each, and fans still argue about which is the best—but both include the reggae hit "Police and Thieves," as well as the great "London's Burning" and "I'm So Bored with the USA."

Halfway to Paradise
Billy Fury | 1961

Pre-Beatles teen idol Billy Fury from Liverpool had a tough-yet-vulnerable image that was perfect for this steaming ballad of emotional and sexual frustration.

Paint It Black
The Rolling Stones | 1966

Mick Jagger was in full brooding, doleful mood over the swirling rhythms and sitar backdrop of this hit—a bundle of laughs, no. Riveting, yes.

Blue Suede Shoes
Carl Perkins | 1956

"Blue Suede Shoes" was the classic echo-drenched sound of Sun Records, Memphis. Rockabilly composer Perkins missed out on superstardom, but was compensated with the royalties that came in when the song became a massive worldwide hit for Elvis Presley.

Ten
Pearl Jam | 1991

While rooted in the classic rock of the '70s, the new-age punk approach of Pearl Jam endeared them to a whole new generation of disaffected American youth in the '90s. In many ways, their debut album *Ten* defined what the Seattle-based "grunge" movement was all about.

The Night Has a Thousand Eyes
Bobby Vee | 1962

Here's a strangely poetic lyric from a singer often unfairly considered a poor man's Buddy Holly, and Vee handled this song with a strident authority only hinted at in his other hits. "So remember when you tell those little white lies..."

To Know Him Is to Love Him
The Teddy Bears | 1958

Phil Spector was still in high school when he put together The Teddy Bears with two classmates, and came up with this all-time teen tearjerker, the title of which he took from the inscription on his late father's gravestone.

Blank Generation
Richard Hell and the Voidoids | 1976

A prototype for punks everywhere, New Yorker Richard Hell wore torn clothes and had spiked hair before anyone else, and the title of this remarkable and innovative track became a calling card for the whole phenomenon.

Anarchy in the U.K.
Sex Pistols | 1976

Anarchy is saying a four-letter word on primetime TV, or wearing a ripped t-shirt, or a safety-pin earring. We might laugh now, but the Sex Pistols' largely contrived anger struck a chord—one of the few they could play—with a generation. And it was like nothing that had gone before.

Surf City
Jan and Dean | 1963

Rivaled only by the Beach Boys in the surfin' stakes, LA high school pals Jan and Dean topped the charts with this ultimate celebration of the sun-kissed lifestyle.

Home of the Brave
Bonnie and the Treasures | 1965

A real bit of teen angst—in fact a protest song of sorts—about a young girl agonizing over her boyfriend being suspended from school because of the length of his hair! Rebel, rebel indeed.

Summertime Blues
Eddie Cochran | 1958

This infectious song about the woes of a broke teenager was a hit with young Americans and Brits alike. Cochran was one of rock's real figures of rebellion in the '50s, and a fine guitar player, who sadly died in a car smash in England in 1960.

Manic Monday
The Bangles | 1985

Popular LA girl group The Bangles smashed the U.S. and the U.K. charts with "Manic Monday." Their breakthrough hit, this teen anthem was written especially for the group by Prince under the pseudonym Christopher.

Hey Joe
The Jimi Hendrix Experience | 1966

Originally a minor hit for LA group The Leaves, the atmospheric bass and blistering guitar lines on this track introduced the public to Jimi Hendrix—and what an introduction!

Moonlighting
Leo Sayer | 1975

An up-tempo elopement if ever there was one, as a pair of young English runaways head for Gretna Green just over the Scottish border to get married without their parents' consent. It seems more weekend joyride than high drama, but is a great record all the same.

Heartbreak Hotel
Elvis Presley | 1956

The record that catapulted Elvis—and his unique brand of rock-'n'-roll—into world dominance was, unexpectedly, a dark, brooding number full of echo-chamber menace and bluesy guitar and piano. This was the sound that was to take a whole generation down to the end of Lonely Street, and they'd never, ever come back.

My Generation
The Who | 1965

This infamous stuttering, amphetamine-fuelled Mod rock anthem famously declared, "Hope I die before I get old" on behalf of teen rebels through the ages.

Remember You're Mine
Pat Boone | 1957

She's going away, he's left at home, and all high-school sweethearts know that summer vacation's a prime time for holiday romance—a word of warning to all and an ideal vehicle for Pat Boone's rich baritone voice.

Needles and Pins
Jackie DeShannon | 1963

"Needles and Pins" later became a much bigger hit for Liverpool's The Searchers, but this original version, written by Jack Nitzsche and Sonny Bono, captured the ache in the lyrics far better.

Complicated
Avril Lavigne | 2002

Teen-diva Avril Lavigne, whose defiant skater-punk image was a reaction to the bland sexuality of pop princesses like Britney Spears, produced some tough-sounding pop that belied her tender years. "Complicated" from the album *Let Go* is her most successful song to date.

School's Out
Alice Cooper | 1972

Heavy metal showman Cooper celebrated rebellious teen emancipation on his biggest hit "School's Out"—like, um, it's the summer vacation, guys.

Endless Sleep
Jody Reynolds | 1958

"The night was black, rain fallin' down...." So opens one of the great "doom discs"—possibly *the* greatest—of the rock-'n'-roll era. The narrator follows his drowned girlfriend into the sea to join her "in an endless sleep," with no happy ending. Heavy stuff.

Tell Laura I Love Her
Ray Peterson | 1960

This is the tragic saga of love-struck Tommy who enters a stock car race because the prize money would be just enough to buy his girl that ring..."As they pulled him from the twisted wreck, with his dying breath they heard him say..."

Heaven Knows, I'm Miserable Now
The Smiths | 1984

British rock group The Smiths were the ultimate teen-angst band in the '80s. On this track, singer Morrissey's bored-in-my-shabby-studio-apartment stance struck a somber chord with disenchanted youth and gave The Smiths a cult following in the U.K. and the U.S.

Sheena Is a Punk Rocker
The Ramones | 1977

Way ahead of their spiky-headed British counterparts, The Ramones' breakneck tracks were the template for punk powerpop forever after.

C'mon Everybody
Eddie Cochran | 1959

This teen anthem, a bigger hit in the U.K. than in Eddie Cochran's native America, was his call to a teen party that you just knew would end up a riot—"Now the house is empty, the folks are gone..."

Our Day Will Come
Ruby and the Romantics | 1963

A sweeping, dramatic vocal-group opus written by Bob Hillard and Mort Garson, "Our Day Will Come" was later covered by Frankie Valli, The Carpenters, and most recently Christina Aguilera.

As Tears Go By
Marianne Faithfull | 1964

Though credited in later years with more than one critically acclaimed comeback, Marianne Faithfull is still remembered by many as the winsome-looking schoolgirl who first nervously warbled her way through this Mick Jagger and Keith Richard song on U.K. TV screens.

Will You Love Me Tomorrow?
The Shirelles | 1961

From talented all-girl quartet The Shirelles came the definitive version of the Gerry Goffin and Carole King ballad describing the inevitable self-doubt of young love: "Is this a lasting treasure or just a moment's pleasure?"

Sixteen Candles
The Crests | 1958

Legend has it that this Brooklyn outfit were originally spotted singing on the subway. The first of the "Italian" school of New York vocal groups, their debut came with this essential piece of school-kid schmaltz.

Pump It Up
Elvis Costello | 1978

The most memorable track from the album *This Year's Model*, this classic song is post-punk power pop with a vengeance—"List'ning to the Muzak."

Don't Let Me Get Me
Pink | 2002

With this bold and brash ode to self-loathing, Pink—aka feisty young American singer Alicia Moore—poked fun at the music industry, herself, and her chart rivals: "Tired of being compared to damn Britney Spears / She's so pretty, that just ain't me." And angst-ridden teens the world over just loved her for it.

I Can Never Go Home Anymore
The Shangri-Las | 1965

Trust The Shangri-Las, and the genius of their producer George "Shadow" Morton, to come up with the ultimate "she's leaving home" drama, with the mother dying from the heartbreak...

Girls Just Want to Have Fun
Cyndi Lauper | 1983

Kooky-looking Cyndi Lauper's warmly aggressive style was a forerunner to the assertive teen spirit of the likes of Avril Lavigne and Pink nearly 20 years later, and her 1983 hit a forthright plea for girl power.

Donna
Ritchie Valens | 1958

"Donna" was an archetypal teen-angst drama from Mexican-American rock-'n'-roll pioneer Valens, who died in the same plane crash as Buddy Holly and the Big Bopper the following year.

Love Will Tear Us Apart
Joy Division | 1980

With its punk meets synth melancholy, this classic track of young love gone horribly wrong gained teen cult status the world over. It was made all the more poignant following frontman Ian Curtis' tragic suicide just months after it was recorded. What makes this song particularly effective is that you can dance to it, never mind the subject matter.

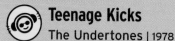

Teenage Kicks
The Undertones | 1978

The pop-punk quartet from Northern Ireland came up with what many consider *the* teen anthem of that, or indeed any, era. "Are teenage dreams so hard to beat?"

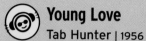

Young Love
Tab Hunter | 1956

Screen and TV teen idol Tab Hunter had a Number One hit with this cheesy slice of sentimental schlock—"They say for every boy and girl, there's just one love in this whole world." "Young Love" is so bad, it's weirdly fascinating.

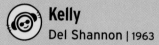

Kelly
Del Shannon | 1963

Following on from the huge success of his rock-'n'-roll hit "Runaway," falsetto-voiced Shannon recorded this anguished teen sob story as the flipside to the single "Two Kinds of Teardrops."

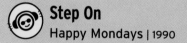

Step On
Happy Mondays | 1990

The Mondays' fusion of club culture and the British "Madchester" sound of the '90s made this a cult anthem in student bars across the U.K. and beyond. The funky feel and the cheeky naughtiness of Shaun Ryder and co. captured the moment perfectly.

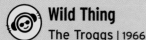 Wild Thing
The Troggs | 1966

Musically basic, Neanderthal even, but a huge hit that went to
Number One in the U.S. "Wild Thing" has since been covered by
everyone from Jimi Hendrix to R.E.M. In attitude, this was punk
before its time.

Born Too Late
The Poni-Tails | 1958

As their name implies, The Poni-Tails were a cutesy-pie high school
girl group emoting youthful yearnings for someone at least a whole
year older!

Send Me Some Lovin'
Little Richard | 1957

A slightly slower Little Richard song than was the norm, this
flipside to the hit "Lucille" has him in fine blues-shouting form with
a rock-'n'-roll adoption of the classic 32-bar pop song format.

Roll Over Beethoven
Electric Light Orchestra | 1973

Though not as effective in its simplicity as either the Chuck Berry
original or the subsequent version by The Beatles, ELO's take on
this rock-'n'-roll classic has to be included purely for the audacious
use of the first few notes of Beethoven's "Fifth Symphony" as an
introduction. Cheeky.

Should I Stay or Should I Go
The Clash | 1982

Contrary to the band's original purist punk ethos, this most familiar
of their singles from the best-selling album *Combat Rock* gained its
widest audience via a 1991 TV commercial.

Born to Be with You
The Chordettes | 1956

Teen romance was personified by the close harmonies of female
pop vocalists The Chordettes on the American Number Five "Born
to Be with You." Don't knock it.

Chinese Rocks
The Heartbreakers | 1977

Co-written by Dee Dee Ramone, this track by The Heartbreakers
typified the junkie-rock that characterized a drug-fuelled hardcore
fringe of punk and post-punk bands. Scarily sad, but true.

Like a Rolling Stone
Bob Dylan | 1965

Of all the anthems that Bob Dylan produced when he was *the*
voice of the young, this is the one that still has (now middle-aged)
audiences in nostalgic reverie. In 2004, *Rolling Stone* magazine
voted it the greatest song of all time, saying, "No other pop song
has so thoroughly challenged and transformed the commercial laws
and artistic conventions of its time, for all time."

Give Us Your Blessings
The Shangri-Las | 1965

Producer George "Shadow" Morton, famed for his seagulls and motorbike roars, didn't lay the sound effects on any thicker than in this tale of two absconding lovers. We've got wedding bells, pouring rain, thunder and lightning, and of course that fatal car smash.

It's My Party
Lesley Gore | 1963

Teen queen Lesley Gore's early '60s hit has become a timeless catchphrase that has far outlived the rest of her repertoire, "...and I'll cry if I want to."

Tammy
Debbie Reynolds | 1957

Wholesome young actress and archetypal girl-next-door Debbie Reynolds had a hit with this treacly chart topper taken from the teen-flick *Tammy and the Bachelor* that Reynolds also starred in.

God Save the Queen
Sex Pistols | 1977

The tabloid shock-horror reaction to the Pistols' debut in '76 was matched only by the outrage at their musically trashing the Queen's Silver Jubilee the following year with the release of this single. The band, their manager, and several others were arrested after performing this anti-establishment punk song on a boat on the River Thames in London during the celebrations.

Fight the Power
Public Enemy | 1989

One of the most influential rap groups of all time, this controversial hip hop outfit was called upon to pen the theme track to the equally talked-about Spike Lee movie *Do the Right Thing*. "Fight the Power" drew criticism for its attacks on iconic American figures but, as with most of Public Enemy's output, criticism didn't seem to harm things any.

New Rose
The Damned | 1976

High on energy, low on content, this track is memorable if only as the first single by a British punk group. The band quickly followed up their success by releasing the first U.K. punk album *Damned, Damned, Damned*.

I Love How You Love Me
The Paris Sisters | 1961

Directly inspired by The Teddy Bears' "To Know Him Is to Love Him" of 1958, this youthful expression of true love was written by Barry Mann and Larry Kolber and masterminded by Phil Spector—who had been part of The Teddy Bears while he was still in high school.

Rhythm of the Rain
The Cascades | 1962

Another song about teenage heartbreak, but this time from an all-male group, the aptly-named one-hit wonders The Cascades. In this ballad, with its rainstorm sound effects, the love prospects are as bleak as the weather.

 Beautiful
Christina Aguilera | 2002

On one of the most controversial videos of 2002, Christina embraced alternative lifestyles by featuring gay men kissing, transvestites, and every other minority group destined to shock Middle America to its core. And the song? A beautiful ballad with an inspirational message penned by Linda Perry of 4 Non Blondes fame.

Past, Present, and Future
The Shangri-Las | 1966

Once voted by Pete Townshend as among the top ten greatest pop records ever, and elsewhere described as "possibly the most extraordinary record ever made." The Shangri-Las surpassed even their own teen-trauma classics "Leader of the Pack" and "I Can Never Go Home Anymore" with this post-rape psychodrama monologue voiced over Beethoven's "Moonlight Sonata." Chilling.

CUTTING EDGE

Certain moments in music are cutting edge by virtue of being genuinely innovative—Elvis' debut single, The Beach Boys' *Pet Sounds* album, The Sugarhill Gang with the first rap hit, almost anything you care to name by The Beatles—whereas others, by their nature, are simply on the experimental edge of things. The latter include avant-garde adventures in sound from artists as varied as John Cage, Talking Heads, John Cale, and Sonic Youth. Then there are all those that fall somewhere in between, pioneering performers ranging from Roxy Music to The Raveonettes, Jimi Hendrix to Pulp, who redrew the musical boundaries a bit further in this direction or that. Every one of these extraordinary artists produced that wonderful sense of surprise that only music at its very best can evoke.

Pet Sounds

The Beach Boys | 1966

With the groundbreaking "God Only Knows," "Sloop John B," and "Wouldn't It Be Nice"–and "Good Vibrations" recorded at the same sessions although not featured on the album–*Pet Sounds* was undoubtedly The Beach Boys' finest hour.

Cops on Our Tail

The Raveonettes | 2002

Retro-punks from Denmark, The Raveonettes emerged onto the new garage-rock scene in 2002 with the release of *Whip It On*. On this track, the duo of Sune Rose Wagner and Sharin Foo take us down that frantic highway to the place "where all the lights shine on," with shades of The Velvet Underground.

It's Like That

Run-DMC | 1983

As the first rap crew to have a worldwide profile, Run DMC's debut single was of huge significance. With its street-jargon lyrics laid over scratch sounds and a drum machine, "It's Like That" was way ahead of its time.

The Rise and Fall of Ziggy Stardust and the Spiders from Mars

David Bowie | 1972

In his masterpiece concept album, David Bowie created a whole onstage persona around the extra-terrestrial starman character Ziggy. With crucial numbers including "Starman," "Ziggy Stardust," and "Rock 'n' Roll Suicide," this record was a landmark for both David Bowie and British rock.

The Slim Shady LP
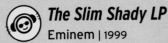

Eminem | 1999

With track titles including "Guilty Conscience," "Brain Damage," and "Just Don't Give a Fuck," this was the album—named after Eminem's alter ego Slim Shady—that finally dragged rap, kicking and four-letter screaming, into the music mainstream.

Eight Miles High

The Byrds | 1966

Allegedly about an airplane flight, David Crosby admitted folk rockers The Byrds "were stoned" when they wrote this innovative, trippy evocation of where heads were going in the summer of 1966.

Tubular Bells
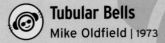

Mike Oldfield | 1973

Mike Oldfield's self-written 49-minute instrumental, on which he played all the music himself with over 1000 overdubs, was a worldwide hit. It was also a major commercial factor in the launch of Virgin Records and, arguably, Richard Branson's subsequent business empire.

4'33"

John Cage | 1952

The sound of silence! The work of influential avant-garde composer John Cage is concerned with the nature of music as a series of sounds and the silences in between. This celebrated piece involved a pianist sitting silently in front of a piano for four minutes and 33 seconds—a landmark in experimental music. And yes, this track and other "silent" compositions *are* available to download from various music Web sites!

Drive
The Cars | 1984

The Cars were American new-wavers who blended an art-rock attitude with pop sensibilities. Their hit single "Drive" gained an audience of millions when it was featured as the musical motif for the Live Aid charity concerts in 1985, asking "Who's gonna drive you home tonight?"

Oliver's Army
Elvis Costello | 1979

From his *Armed Forces* album, this anthemic anti-military sing-along written by the always-challenging Declan McManus, aka Elvis Costello, is definitely "...here to stay."

Common People
Pulp | 1995

Jarvis Cocker's epic tale of a poor little rich girl, who "slums it" for kicks, was apparently based on someone he knew at college—a true classic of the Britpop era.

Hey Joe / Piss Factory
Patti Smith | 1974

Punk poetess Smith's debut single doubled an aggressive version of Hendrix's "Hey Joe" with a flipside written some years before. "Piss Factory" was a nihilistic view of industrial work based on Smith's own experience of factory life during a college vacation. A stunning harbinger of things to come.

That's All Right
Elvis Presley | 1954

As cutting edge as it gets, Elvis' debut on Sun Records—with a song by bluesman Arthur "Big Boy" Crudup—was a synthesis of white country music and black blues that was simply unheard of at the time, and it became the template for future rock-'n'-roll.

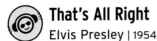

Star Spangled Banner
Jimi Hendrix | 1969

A highlight of the Woodstock festival, Jimi Hendrix's anarchic take on the American national anthem was as technically mind-blowing as it was audacious.

Rapper's Delight
The Sugarhill Gang | 1979

A stream of verbalizing that was a sensation at the time, "Rapper's Delight," released by the New Jersey-based hip-hop label Sugarhill Records, was the very first rap record to become a hit.

O Superman
Laurie Anderson | 1981

Avant-garde performance artist Laurie Anderson's work centers on her obsession with electronics, technology, and the political ramifications thereof. Her eight-minute 1981 single was voted "most likely to clear dance floors" by disco-dominated music fans, but still made it to Number Two in the U.K. charts!

Waiting for Your Taxi
Ian Dury and the Blockheads | 1979

From his *Do It Yourself* album, this was a quirky track—even by Ian Dury's often off-the-wall standards—full of sound effects and early morning atmosphere.

Strange Brew
Cream | 1967

The surreal lyrics written by bassist Jack Bruce and poet Pete Brown fused perfectly with Eric Clapton's soaring guitar and Ginger Baker's furious drumming on this track, recorded before the super-trio overindulged themselves musically and otherwise.

The Model / Computer Love
Kraftwerk | 1981

The pioneering German electric techno art rock group Kraftwerk had a surprise U.K. chart topper with this double-sided power plant pop hit.

Songs from Liquid Days
Philip Glass | 1986

Highly influential minimalist Philip Glass—his work has influenced Laurie Anderson, Brian Eno, and David Byrne, among others—was the first composer since Stravinsky to sign an exclusive contract with the prestigious CBS Masterworks label. His third album for them was the song collection *Songs from Liquid Days*, which featured songs by Anderson, Byrne, Paul Simon, and Suzanne Vega, sung by Linda Ronstadt and Janis Pendarvis.

All Tomorrow's Parties
The Velvet Underground | 1967

Nico, the *chanteuse* who was "attached" to The Velvet Underground during the days when Andy Warhol was their manager, provided the haunting vocals alongside John Cale's droning viola in this doomy track from their debut album.

Music for Airports
Brian Eno | 1978

Along with *Music for Films*, this album was electro music pioneer Brian Eno's exploration of the stark landscapes of "Musak," elevating its mundane instrumental qualities to the newly conceived status of "ambient" music.

Porcupine
Echo and the Bunnymen | 1983

Vocalist and guitarist Ian McCulloch could be seen as a post-punk Jim Morrison for the '80s, performing angst-driven songs on this album with often frowningly serious intent. Apparently, "Echo" was the name of the band's drum machine!

In Every Dream Home a Heartache
Roxy Music | 1973

Bryan Ferry's art school background—where he studied under pop art pioneer Richard Hamilton—is well in evidence on this musical collage of advertising copy. This song from the *For Your Pleasure* album is a sinister ode to consumerism centered on the "perfect companion" of an inflatable woman. Creepy.

Marquee Moon
Television | 1977

Formed in 1973, Tom Verlaine's group was not so much pre-punk as pre-New Wave. This, the surreally sinister ten-minute title track from their debut album, had to be split across two sides of a single when it was released.

The Stooges
The Stooges | 1969

On an album way ahead of its time, The Stooges, led by innovative proto-punk Iggy Pop, voiced the urban angst that would later be associated with punk on tracks like "1969" and "No Fun," which were covered by The Sisters of Mercy and Sex Pistols respectively.

Electro-Shock Blues
The Eels | 1998

Quirky, gloomy, arresting, and disturbing—just some of the words that immediately come to mind to describe the second album from the avant-garde LA band. It featured such titles as "Going to Your Funeral," "My Descent into Madness," "Hospital Food," and "The Medication Is Wearing Off," mostly based on lead vocalist and songwriter Mark Oliver Everett's own personal tragedies.

Stop Breaking Down
The White Stripes | 2001

From latter-day power punks Meg and Jack White, this track from their debut album, simply entitled *The White Stripes*, is a hitting-you-between-the-eyes version of a vintage Robert Johnson song. Hard-edged blues for the 21st century.

More Songs about Buildings and Food
Talking Heads | 1978

The Heads' second collection, produced by techno musician Brian Eno, formerly of Roxy Music fame, was pivotal in the development of the avant-garde tendencies of the band's frontman David Byrne.

Tainted Love
Soft Cell | 1981

A huge hit on both sides of the Atlantic and beyond, the duo of Marc Almond and David Ball brought underground sensibilities to bear on this Gloria Jones disco favorite, which remains a stylish sing-along to this day.

A Love Supreme
John Coltrane | 1964

A few years ago in San Francisco, I came across the Orthodox African Church of Saint John Coltrane. *A Love Supreme* was the four-part album that, more than any other, inspired such ardent religious devotion among some of his fans—the result of the sax giant's own communion with his god.

Live at the Witch Trials
The Fall | 1979

This debut album from the avant-garde punks from Manchester, England is still considered, by aficionados at least, the best example of vocalist Mark E. Smith's atonal style set against a ruthlessly freeform guitar backing.

Blue Monday

New Order | 1983

"Blue Monday" is regarded as a classic in the annals of electro-pop. With atonal vocals and obscure lyrics, this single reinvented club dance music and triggered the techno revolution to come.

Trout Mask Replica

Captain Beefheart and His Magic Band | 1969

A true eccentric, Captain Beefheart's acknowledged masterpiece was *Trout Mask Replica*, an often-disturbing, experimental collection of 28 weird and wonderful songs, including "Dachau Blues," "The Blimp," and "Old Fart at Play," that hovered between freeform jazz and rock.

Debut

Björk | 1993

Endearingly eccentric Björk debuted with this aptly titled album after first finding fame with a group called The Sugarcubes in her native Iceland. The press loved it, the public loved it, and the quirky-voiced one warbled her way into hearts everywhere.

Heartbreak Hotel

John Cale | 1975

Welsh composer and musician Cale, who graduated from music college and then The Velvet Underground, has been nothing less than eclectic throughout his varied career. His somber take on the Elvis Presley smash "Heartbreak Hotel" sounds as though he was a time-served resident of the place.

West End Girls
Pet Shop Boys | 1985

This massive Pet Shop Boys' hit was the ultimate in electro-pop when it came out, with not a "real" instrument in sight to back the dead-pan vocals and knowing lyrics: "We've got no future, we've got no past, here today, built to last."

EVOL
Sonic Youth | 1986

The uncompromising avant-garde band Sonic Youth came out of the New York "no wave" experimental scene of the late '70s and early '80s. Their *EVOL* album marked the beginning of the band's tongue-in-cheek obsession with Madonna.

Niggers Are Scared of Revolution
The Last Poets | 1970

The Last Poets came out of Harlem in the late '60s, espousing radical lyrics that reflected the militant end of the "black is beautiful" movement. This track, as confrontational as the title suggests, was part of their eponymous debut album and a stark precursor to rap.

Comfortably Numb
Scissor Sisters | 2004

New York gay-scene band Scissor Sisters had a memorable hit in the U.K. with their disco-oriented version of Pink Floyd's meditation on drug-induced anesthesia "Comfortably Numb," much to the chagrin of many Floyd fans.

I Oughta Give You a Shot in the Head for Making Me Live in This Dump
Shivaree | 1999

This album by New York band Shivaree is almost worth listing just for the name of lead singer Ambrosia Parsley and the title of the album itself, but Parsley's taut vocals and in-your-face lyrics make it even more worthwhile.

The B-52's
The B-52's | 1979

Postmodern before its time, The B-52's debut album was camp-kitsch electro trash, but ultimately, an affectionate celebration of suburban Americana.

Buffalo Stance
Neneh Cherry | 1988

Half-Swedish and with model good looks, Neneh Cherry is the stepdaughter of legendary jazz trumpeter Don Cherry and a former punk collaborator. She married smart rap and top pop hooks on this irresistible track—taken from her *Raw Like Sushi* album—that made it into all the end-of-year editors' picks.

Why Does It Always Rain on Me?
Travis | 1999

One of the pioneers of the new millennium's most successful genre—melancholy indie balladry—Travis saw the old century out with a bang. This track helped the boys from Scotland shift millions of copies of their album *The Man Who*, though they've since been overtaken by the likes of Coldplay.

Hong Kong Garden
Siouxsie and the Banshees | 1978

Despite travelogue "Chinese" references seemingly inspired by
Siouxsie's local takeaway, instrumentally—and in its overall effect—
this was one of the most atmospheric singles to be released in the
wake of punk.

Jack Your Body
Steve "Silk" Hurley | 1987

In 1987, super-producer Steve "Silk" Hurley brought house music to
the mainstream with this simple track highlighting the new dance
movement emerging from the Chicago clubs. So massive it
guaranteed Hurley remixing work for years to come, while setting
the standard for more than a decade of dance.

Gravest Hits
The Cramps | 1979

The influential, crazy-looking rockabilly revivalists—with lead singer
Lux Interior doing the over-the-top Elvis bit to the extreme—
included this explanation in the liner notes to their five-song debut
EP: "In the spring of 1976, The Cramps began to fester in a NYC
apartment. Without fresh air or natural light, the group developed
its uniquely mutant strain of rock-'n'-roll aided only by the sickly
blue rays of late night TV."

SONGSMITHS

There would be no great songs without great songwriters—
from composers George Gershwin and Cole Porter, and
songwriting teams Rodgers and Hart, Leiber and Stoller,
and Lennon and McCartney to the solo phenomenon of the
singer-songwriter, pioneered by folk performers, and, more
specifically, Bob Dylan. The best lyricists can be compared
to our greatest poets, and it's about time we honored those
men and women who have given us some of the greatest
pop songs ever composed. Let's not forget those most
talented of singers, who have unraveled these magnificent
lyrics and made them come alive. Interpreting a lyric is an
art form in itself—we only have to listen to Frank Sinatra or
Ella Fitzgerald's versions of old Broadway standards to see
that. But it's the song itself that is so unforgettable and so
central to the popular music tradition.

Johnny B. Goode
Chuck Berry | 1958

This was one of the first anthems of rock-'n'-roll written and performed by the first poet of rock-'n'-roll, Chuck Berry. It is the semi-autobiographical story of a poor boy who hits the big time because "he could play a guitar just like a-ringing a bell"—the rock-'n'-roll version of the American dream.

Jagged Little Pill
Alanis Morissette | 1995

With her hugely successful debut album Morissette created the mold for female singer-songwriters in the '90s—aggressive, though often self-deprecating vocals with production values just sophisticated enough to ensure pop accessibility.

Graceland
Paul Simon | 1986

A father and son, bittersweet memories, the Mississippi Delta "shining like a National guitar," and a trip to the King's home, Paul Simon's "Graceland" is sheer poetry.

Come Away with Me
Norah Jones | 2002

Velvet-voiced Norah Jones asserted herself as *the* voice of the first decade of the 21st century with her debut *Come Away With Me*. The album featured material from sources as diverse as Hank Williams and Hoagy Carmichael together with her own well-crafted compositions, which included the best-selling title track.

Spanish Harlem
Ben E. King | 1960

One of the greatest songwriting teams ever, Leiber and Stoller proved they could make romance out of even the most mundane of urban settings on this classic track, which became King's first solo hit. Pure magic.

Tracy Chapman
Tracy Chapman | 1988

A singer-songwriter of socially committed songs, Tracy Chapman's sensational debut album rocketed up the charts after her stunning appearance at the televised tribute concert for Nelson Mandela.

Lola
The Kinks | 1970

"Lola" was one of The Kinks' finest offerings. Songwriter and vocalist Ray Davies of The Kinks has tackled some very un-rock-'n'-roll subject matters in his time, not least on this track concerning a young guy's encounter with a transvestite, "She walked like a woman and talked like a man..."

Visions of Johanna
Bob Dylan | 1966

His 1966 album *Blonde on Blonde* represented Dylan at his lyrical peak. The single "Visions of Johanna," overflowing with richly evocative imagery, well substantiates the view that Dylan was a major poetic voice of the 20th century: "Mona Lisa must have had the Highway Blues, you can see by the way she smiles."

I Shot the Sheriff
Bob Marley | 1973

This was reggae as narrative created by the master of the genre, Bob Marley. Taken from Marley's *Burnin'* album, "I Shot the Sheriff" was also famously covered a year later by Eric Clapton, becoming Clapton's first American Number One.

Days
Kirsty MacColl | 1989

Talented singer-songwriter MacColl had a hit with her affectionate reading of this 1968 song written by Ray Davies of the Kinks: "Thank you for the days...."

Mountain Greenery
Mel Tormé | 1956

Jazz singer Mel Tormé sang the definitive version of this Rodgers and Hart classic from the '20s. They simply don't write lines like "Simple cooking means more than French cuisines, I've a banquet planned which is sandwiches and beans" any more.

Non Je Ne Regrette Rien
Edith Piaf | 1960

The husky, melancholy voice of the diminutive "little sparrow" and her emotionally charged delivery made Piaf *the* musical toast of France throughout the late '40s and '50s, and a huge international star. This song, written especially for Piaf by songwriters Charles Dumont and Michel Vaucaire, will forever be her signature song and she certainly made it her own.

Mother

John Lennon | 1970

"You had me, but I never had you"—Lennon's pleading flashback to a childhood in which he was brought up, albeit lovingly, without his parents. "Mother" was the first track of his highly personalized, minimalist-sounding album *Plastic Ono Band*.

Light My Fire

Jose Feliciano | 1968

Feliciano's cover of this classic Doors' song—written by guitarist Robby Krieger—won him a Grammy Award. His soulful delivery struck a perfect balance with the Latin-folk rock flavor of the music.

Ingénue

k.d. lang | 1992

In her million-selling album *Ingénue*, Canadian singer-songwriter k.d. lang—whose stance as a "country" singer has always been highly individual—completely ignored any stylistic barriers between country and the music mainstream.

Get Away from Me

Nellie McKay | 2004

With a perfectly pitched voice, jazzy piano technique, and songwriting skills that have drawn comparisons to the great Cole Porter, Nellie McKay's first album, recorded while she was still in her teens, suggests she could become a serious phenomenon, regardless of the hype.

Highlands
Bob Dylan | 1997

At sixteen-and-a-half-minutes, "Highlands" was a latter-day epic from influential songwriter Bob Dylan. When asked by a record executive whether there would be a radio-friendly short version of the song, Dylan allegedly replied that this *was* the short version!

Manhattan
Ella Fitzgerald | 1956

Rodgers and Hart's romantic evocation of a 1920s New York that never really was has never been interpreted better than by Ella Fitzgerald—pure magic.

Me Myself I
Joan Armatrading | 1980

Singer-songwriter Armatrading's deep, resonant voice belied the intimacy of most of her lyrics—"I sit here by myself / And you know I love it..." This single also marked a move away from an acoustic ambience to a heavier rock setting.

Bridge over Troubled Water
Simon and Garfunkel | 1970

Paul Simon and Art Garfunkel were one of the world's most successful duos, and this album, despite the slightly schmaltzy title track, was full of masterful Simon songs. The album included possibly their best ever track, "The Boxer," as well as the hit singles "Baby Driver," "El Condor Pasa," and "Cecelia."

Let's Just Get Naked
Joan Osbourne | 1995

Sounding like a female version of Lou Reed from his Velvet Underground days, Joan Osbourne's dark delivery and wired accompaniment on this self-penned single is as morosely magnificent as anything you're likely to hear.

September Song
Sarah Vaughan | 1954

One of the greatest interpreters of popular songs, "Sassy" was never in better form than on this glorious rendering of Kurt Weill's "September Song," on which she was supported by the great Clifford Brown on the trumpet.

Ode to Billy Joe
Bobbie Gentry | 1967

In Gentry's "Ode to Billy Joe," the tragedy of a teen romance gone horribly wrong is spelled out amid casual chat—"pass the biscuits please"—around a small-town family dinner table. Sheer pop poetry.

American Pie
Don McLean | 1971

There are whole websites dedicated to unraveling the mystery of this song's lyrics, but suffice to say, it was clearly inspired by the deaths of Buddy Holly, Ritchie Valens, and the Big Bopper in an airplane crash. At the time of release, it also clearly struck a chord with a war-torn America eager for the nostalgia of "good ol' boys drinkin' whiskey and rye."

Loser
Beck | 1994

This is a fine example of the folk-punk style central to New York's "anti-folk" scene. Californian songwriter Beck's apprenticeship on the streets of N.Y. as a busker shone through on this low-tech hit.

Here Comes the Sun
Richie Havens | 1971

A fine songwriter in his own right, it was Richie Havens' uncomplicated folk approach to other people's material that first brought him to the attention of audiences in the late '60s. Among a wealth of successful albums, this cover of a Beatles' song was his only hit single.

Games People Play
Joe South | 1969

Joe South's songwriting credits include "Down in the Boondocks," "Rose Garden," and "Walk a Mile in My Shoes." But his biggest hit was this much-covered soft-rock classic, which won a Grammy Award for Song of the Year in 1970.

Suzanne Vega
Suzanne Vega | 1985

Although her folk style was initially dismissed by some critics, Vega's low-key but highly literate songs clearly struck a chord with the record-buying public at a time when singer-songwriters were generally considered unfashionable. This, her debut album, is often still considered her best, but she is better known for the follow-up *Solitude Standing*, which included the hit "Tom's Diner."

You're the Top
Anita O'Day | 1956

Jazz singer Anita O'Day gave us one of the finest interpretations of this classic song by the great songwriter Cole Porter from the Broadway musical *Anything Goes:* "You're the Nile, you're the Tower of Pisa, you're the smile on the Mona Lisa."

Ain't Misbehavin'
Fats Waller | 1929

Waller was a huge star in the '30s and many of his songs became standards. None more so than "Ain't Misbehavin'," which he wrote while serving time in prison for not making his alimony payments.

Poetry Man
Phoebe Snow | 1974

Singer-songwriter Snow began performing around New York's Greenwich Village in the early '70s, initially setting her poems to music. In 1975 she had a huge hit on her hands with "Poetry Man," the possibly autobiographical account of having a "giggling teenage crush" on an already-married poet.

All I Wanna Do
Sheryl Crow | 1994

Former session vocalist Sheryl Crow won two Grammy Awards with this song, although the lyrics were actually taken from a poem by Vermont poet Wyn Cooper. From her debut album *Tuesday Night Music Club*, "All I Wanna Do" was the prelude to her tough-sounding brand of country-tinged rock and a string of hit albums.

Sweet Baby James
James Taylor | 1970

One of the most influential examples of singer-songwriter soft rock from the early '70s, James Taylor's second album *Sweet Baby James* ranged in style from the gently rolling blues of "Steamroller" to the sheer poetry of "Fire and Rain."

Power of Love
Jennifer Rush | 1985

Big-voiced Jen (the daughter of an opera singer) became the first female soloist to sell a million copies of a single in the U.K. alone with this favorite sing-along power ballad that she co-wrote.

I Left My Heart in San Francisco
Tony Bennett | 1962

A supreme master of the standard ballad, Tony Bennett's unofficial signature tune was this paean to one of America's greatest cities, "Where little cable cars climb halfway to the stars..." and a travelogue soundtrack standby ever since.

Babylon
David Gray | 2000

David Gray's *White Ladder* album was the surprise hit of the year, making it big through word of mouth—the British singer-songwriter and his acoustic guitar had been continuously working for years before this breakthrough. "Babylon" was one of *the* standout tracks on the album, beloved for its uplifting, beautifully produced, yet gentle feel.

Desolation Row
Bob Dylan | 1965

One of Dylan's many epic pieces, "Desolation Row" is a surrealistic poem set to a Spanish American-tinged melody with lyrics that are often considered his best—"Between the windows of the sea where lovely mermaids flow."

After the Gold Rush
Neil Young | 1970

One of the great ballads of the post-hippie era, "After the Gold Rush" included stunning surreal imagery evoking Canadian singer-songwriter Young's heartfelt melancholy at the shattered dreams of the '60s: "Mother Nature on the run in the 1970s."

What a Diff'rence a Day Makes
Dinah Washington | 1959

Strong-voiced Dinah Washington brought a dynamic jazz and blues feel to a variety of pop standards to telling effect. This single was just about the biggest, and just about the best.

Why
Annie Lennox | 1992

The listening public wondered if Scottish singer Lennox could really pull off a successful solo career without the talented Dave Stewart behind her. But with this track from her debut album *Diva*, her first outside of Eurythmics, she proved she could. However, the video did hark back to those classic iconic videos from her Eurythmics days.

Bad Bad Leroy Brown
Jim Croce | 1973

"The baddest man in the whole damned town" was the subject of the last song, a chart topper, by singer-songwriter Jim Croce before he was killed in a plane crash. He left behind a very impressive legacy of work, much of it released posthumously.

Blue Horse
The Be Good Tanyas | 2000

Curious, and strangely endearing, this debut album put the spotlight on the young Vancouver trio of songbirds and their sometimes flirty, sometimes quirky take on traditional folk and bluegrass music.

Let There Be Love
Nat King Cole and George Shearing | 1962

The pairing of Nat King Cole and pianist George Shearing made for a great album, simply entitled *Nat King Cole Sings / George Shearing Plays*. This hit single, written by Lionel Rand and Ian Grant, was its absolute highlight: "...but most of all please let there be love."

California
Rufus Wainwright | 2002

With a musical pedigree second to none—he is the son of folk music icons Loudon Wainwright III and Kate McGarrigle—and a personal history to make the hairs stand up on your arms, Rufus Wainwright is a singer-songwriter *par excellence*. This song from his *Poses* album was, with its witty lyrics and catchy hooks, immediately fast-tracked to legendary status.

Doo Wop (That Thing)
Lauryn Hill | 1998

Lauryn Hill shone as the voice of hip-hop group The Fugees, alongside Wyclef Jean and Pras Michel in the early '90s. She went on to bag a handful of Grammy Awards for her first self-penned solo outing, *The Miseducation of Lauryn Hill*, from which this single—her best rap hit so far—was taken.

Send in the Clowns
Judy Collins | 1975

This beautiful tearjerker of a song was written by Stephen Sondheim for the show *A Little Night Music*. It is best remembered as this flawless rendition by folk singer Judy Collins, "...there ought to be clowns, well, maybe next year." Timeless.

Across the Universe
Fiona Apple | 1999

With her fragile, almost cracked voice, Fiona Apple's treatment of The Beatles' wistful piece of musical cosmology "Across the Universe" does a seemingly slight song a great justice.

Faith
George Michael | 1987

After he became a global heartthrob alongside Andrew Ridgeley in the pop group Wham!, the world was totally unprepared for the heights George Michael could achieve on his own with a guitar and a leather jacket. "Faith," the standout track from his massive album of the same name, made him a superstar and rose to the Number One spot in the U.S.

Hallelujah
Jeff Buckley | 1994

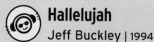

The anthem of anyone who has ever picked up a guitar while under the influence of melancholy, this striking cover of a classic Leonard Cohen song from the son of vocalist Tim Buckley is a masterpiece beloved of lonely boys the world over. Following Buckley's mysterious and untimely death, cult status was assured.

Déjà Vu
Crosby, Stills, Nash, and Young | 1970

Hippie heroes of laidback harmony singing, veterans Dave Crosby of The Byrds, Stephen Stills of Buffalo Springfield, and Graham Nash of The Hollies had their finest hour with this album, with the more caustic Neil Young added to the mix.

Elvis Presley Blues
Gillian Welch | 2001

From her sensational third album *Time (The Revelator)* that somehow managed to fuse folk, country, rock, and blues, this track is Gillian Welch's moving reflection on the last lonely hours of the King of rock-'n'-roll.

Without You
Harry Nilsson | 1971

Harry Nilsson won a Grammy Award for his definitive version of "Without You," written by Pete Ham and Tommy Evans of the group Badfinger. This poignant plea to a departing lover starts simply and builds to a crescendo of emotion that sounds restrained and heartfelt, making it one the most evocative love songs of the '70s– or any other decade for that matter.

Your Song
Elton John | 1970

With Bernie Taupin writing the lyrics and Elton John adding the music, this became a classic love song and it epitomized a songwriting partnership at the absolute height of its powers. "Your Song" was most recently revisited—and rather nicely, too—by Ewan McGregor for the soundtrack to the film *Moulin Rouge*.

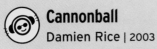

Cannonball
Damien Rice | 2003

Touted as a word-of-mouth hit, Damien Rice's album *O* was actually heavily advertised, which is one of the reasons why the skillful Irish songwriter's haunting ballad "Cannonball" so engrained itself in the public consciousness. Rice managed to bring something new to the singer-songwriter genre and his success seems set to spawn a new generation of melancholy boy balladeers.

music from the movies

Once movies acquired sound in the '20s—heralded by Al Jolson's famous "You ain't heard nothing yet" in *The Jazz Singer*—they became a major force in popular music. The golden age of the Hollywood musical brought the magic of the hit Broadway shows to audiences of millions, while also creating musical spectacles ranging from the escapist Fred Astaire extravaganzas of the '30s to screen classics like *Singin' in the Rain* in the '50s. The classical scores and pop music soundtracks of non-musical films have often proved as enduring as the movies themselves: consider perhaps the timeless themes from *The Big Country* and *Chariots of Fire*. And let's not forget those remarkable scenes—John Travolta and Uma Thurman dancing to Chuck Berry in *Pulp Fiction*, Dennis Hopper and Peter Fonda "Born to Be Wild" on Harley-Davidson motorbikes, or Audrey Hepburn singing "Moon River" in *Breakfast at Tiffany's*—that have become iconic music moments in their own right.

Born to Be Wild
Steppenwolf | 1968

One of the most enduring cinematic images ever is still Dennis Hopper and Peter Fonda in the seminal road movie *Easy Rider* biking across the American landscape "Like a true nature's child" to the tune of "Born to Be Wild."

Well Did You Evah?
Bing Crosby and Frank Sinatra | 1956

Elegantly dressed in tuxedos, Bing Crosby and Frank Sinatra sang together for the first time on the lively duet "Well Did You Evah?" in the immensely popular Cole Porter musical *High Society*—"What a swell party this is!"

Theme from *Jaws*
John Williams | 1975

Soundtrack music can become as familiar as the movie itself, more so sometimes—and that was certainly the case with John Williams' acclaimed suspenseful score for the film *Jaws*. The pulsing throb that heralded the killer shark's approach in Stephen Spielberg's blockbuster said more about the threat just below the waves than the images ever could.

The Bodyguard: Original Soundtrack Album
Whitney Houston | 1992

Kevin Costner may have played the title role in the hit movie about a pop star's bodyguard, but the film was a vehicle for Whitney Houston's singing talents. As well as the massive Number One cover of Dolly Parton's "I Will Always Love You," *The Bodyguard* soundtrack included Houston's hits, "Queen of the Night," "I'm Every Woman," and "I Have Nothing."

The Call of the Faraway Hills
Victor Young | 1953

Along with those from *The Magnificent Seven* and *The Big Country*, the theme from George Stevens' elegiac lone gunfighter drama *Shane*—"The Call of the Faraway Hills" by Victor Young—perfectly typified Hollywood's musical imagery of the West.

Car Wash
Rose Royce | 1976

Disco funk with an edge from the best-selling soundtrack to the ghetto movie comedy of the same name. "Car Wash" was also recently covered by Missy Elliott and Christina Aguilera for the animated movie *Shark Tale*.

Mrs. Robinson
Simon and Garfunkel | 1967

Famous for elegant older woman Ann Bancroft's seduction of a youthful Dustin Hoffman, the rights-of-passage film *The Graduate* also memorably featured this Simon and Garfunkel song dedicated to the lady herself. "Mrs. Robinson" went on to become a Number One hit in 1968.

Round Midnight: Original Motion Picture Soundtrack
Herbie Hancock | 1986

The atmospheric jazz movie *Round Midnight* starred saxophonist Dexter Gordon as a world-weary American musician living in Paris. Based loosely on the experiences of pianist Bud Powell, who was similarly "rediscovered" in the French capital, this is one of the most authentic jazz films ever made—not least because of Herbie Hancock's excellent original soundtrack.

I Wanna Be Loved by You
Marilyn Monroe | 1959

Billy Wilder's comedy *Some Like It Hot* was considered by many to be Marilyn Monroe's finest hour. Starring as Sugar Kane, the ukulele-strumming singer of a '20s all-girl band, Marilyn sang what was to instantly become her trademark number "I Wanna Be Loved by You"–"Boop-boop-de-boop!"

The Best Things in Life Are Free
Luther Vandross and Janet Jackson | 1992

Featuring BBD and Ralph Tresvant, an all-star–if unlikely–cast at the top of their game made a catchy dance record so good it hit the U.K. Top Ten twice. From the *Mo' Money* movie soundtrack, this slice of feel-good fun was a perfect example of modern soul.

Title Theme from *Chariots of Fire*
Vangelis | 1981

Greek composer and keyboard player Vangelis achieved the seemingly impossible by creating hugely effective title music for a film about athletics–*Chariots of Fire*. No one can possibly hear the first few bars of his theme for the opening titles without picturing the athletes running in slow motion across a beach.

Raindrops Keep Fallin' on My Head
B. J. Thomas | 1969

In a delightful comic scene from the Western *Butch Cassidy and the Sundance Kid*, Paul Newman as the outlaw Butch Cassidy frolicked on a bicycle, showing off to love interest Katharine Ross to the unforgettable tune of "Raindrops Keep Fallin' on My Head." Burt Bacharach and Hal David wrote the song especially for the film, which earned them an Oscar and B. J. Thomas a Number One hit.

Stayin' Alive

The Bee Gees | 1977

John Travolta, in his trademark white suit, strutting his stuff to The Bee Gees is *the* enduring image of the disco era—and this was the tune he did it to. The hit film *Saturday Night Fever* was far grittier than either the song or the subject might suggest and it was based on a real dance club in Brooklyn called the 2001 Odyssey.

Also Sprach Zarathustra

Richard Strauss | 1896

The drama of Richard Strauss' classic piece was brought to a much wider audience than the composer could have ever imagined when it was used by Stanley Kubrick as the opening music to his science-fiction epic *2001: A Space Odyssey*.

Secret Love

Doris Day | 1953

A smash hit for Doris Day, "Secret Love" also earned its writers Sammy Fain and Paul Francis Webster an Oscar for Best Original Song when it was released straight from the movie *Calamity Jane*. The actress was at her peak as the feisty frontierswoman "tamed" by Wild Bill Hickok—hardly PC, but pure escapism with a great-sounding soundtrack.

The Girl Can't Help It

Little Richard | 1956

The '50s movie comedy *The Girl Can't Help It* was a satirical look at the music business, and the best rock-'n'-roll film of the era. Fats Domino, Eddie Cochran, and Gene Vincent all made cameo appearances, but nothing bettered seeing hourglass-figured Jayne Mansfield sashaying down the street to Little Richard's title track.

Up Where We Belong
Joe Cocker and Jennifer Warnes | 1982

From the phenomenally successful *An Officer and a Gentleman* soundtrack, this modern pop standard and karaoke favorite truly reflected the soppy nature of the movie. It excellently paired the gravely voice of Mr. Cocker with the lush sounds of Ms. Warnes.

Theme from *Shaft*
Isaac Hayes | 1971

The theme tune to the thriller *Shaft*, composed and performed by Isaac Hayes, became almost a musical template for numerous other "blaxploitation" movies in the early '70s. But Hayes' rippling rhythm under sweeping horns and strings was the first, and the best.

The Man with the Golden Arm: Original Motion Picture Soundtrack
Elmer Bernstein | 1955

Celebrated composer Elmer Bernstein spent more than 50 years writing soundtracks and theme tunes to over 200 movies and TV shows. He wrote the gritty jazz score to *The Man with the Golden Arm*—a stark drama starring Frank Sinatra as a heroin-addict jazz drummer, which was the shock-horror movie sensation of its day.

Jet Song
The Jets | 1961

From the initial aerial view of Manhattan as the camera swooped the cinema audience down to a finger-clicking close-up of the magnificent "Jet Song," *West Side Story* was a musical like no other. The stage show had been a sensation three years earlier, but the Oscar-winning film took the songs of Leonard Bernstein and Stephen Sondheim to a worldwide audience of millions.

You're the One That I Want
John Travolta and Olivia Newton-John | 1978

An effervescent pastiche of teenage life in '50s America, the movie musical *Grease* about the romantic dilemmas of high school students Olivia Newton-John and John Travolta was a huge box office smash. Amid a host of fun, lively musical numbers, John Farrar's "You're the One That I Want" was the film's most potent song.

Theme from *Exodus*
Ernest Gold | 1960

Biblical in mood and scale, this instrumental theme by the award-winning film music composer Ernest Gold was, nevertheless, perfectly appropriate for the movie *Exodus*, concerning the early days of the founding of a modern state of Israel.

Big Rock Candy Mountain
Harry McClintock | 1928

Harry "Haywire Mac" McClintock's hobo classic was just one of the many bluegrass and old-time music gems on the soundtrack to the 2000 film *O Brother, Where Art Thou?* The Coen Brothers' movie was loosely based on Homer's *The Odyssey* and set in the American South during the Depression-hit '30s.

Beat Street Breakdown
Grandmaster Melle Mel and the Furious Five | 1984

Highlighting a "breaking" battle between the Rock Steady Crew and the New York City Breakers, *Beat Street* was a movie celebration of the break dancing craze that evolved as part of hip-hop street culture in the late '70s and early '80s. The best-known track from the popular soundtrack was "Beat Street Breakdown" by one of the pioneers of hip-hop, MC Melle Mel, aka Melvin Glover.

The Sound of Music
Julie Andrews | 1965

Certainly one of the most successful movie musicals of all time, *The Sound of Music*'s most famous scene was of Julie Andrews spinning around on an alpine hilltop with her arms outstretched and singing Rodgers and Hammerstein's title track—and that is how the actress will be forever remembered.

Rhapsody in Blue
George Gershwin | 1924

From the opening clarinet glissando, George Gershwin's 16-minute piece became the perfect musical tribute to New York as it accompanied stunning black-and-white images of the city one critic said Woody Allen was "born to make films about" following his 1979 film comedy *Manhattan*.

Theme from *M Squad*
Count Basie and His Band | 1958

As tough cop Lee Marvin hunted down criminals among the alleyways and rooftops of the big city, Count Basie and his band roared away in the background with this instrumental theme to the popular '50s TV series *M Squad*.

Paris, Texas: Original Motion Picture Soundtrack
Ry Cooder | 1984

Guitarist and composer Ry Cooder's slide guitar haunted the atmospheric but desolate Wim Wenders' movie *Paris, Texas*. The best known of his many film scores, the music from *Paris, Texas* became something of a template for "wide open spaces" road movie soundtracks and TV ads ever since.

Singin' in the Rain
Gene Kelly | 1952

Gene Kelly's glorious rain-soaked, joy-filled song and dance routine to the classic title song of the much-loved MGM musical *Singin' in the Rain* has become one of the truly iconic sequences in Hollywood cinema: "Doo-dloo-doo-doo-doo..."

Love Is All Around
Wet Wet Wet | 1994

From the soundtrack to the hit British movie *Four Weddings and a Funeral*, Wet Wet Wet's soulful U.K. chart topper was a cover of the 1967 hit by The Troggs. A marvelous pop song in both versions.

I Believe I Can Fly
R. Kelly | 1996

R. Kelly emerged from the "new jack swing" era as a producer and vocalist to watch out for. He certainly didn't hesitate to slap on the sentimentality with this inspirational ode to believing in the power of your dreams. A far cry from his usual sexed-up delivery, this schmaltz-drenched single from the movie *Space Jam* is Kelly's most successful to date.

Walk on the Wild Side
Brook Benton | 1962

Elmer Bernstein's theme *Walk on the Wild Side*, performed by soul singer Brook Benton, delivered more of a punch than the much-heralded film of the same name about a New Orleans prostitute. As did jazz legend Jimmy Smith's strident Hammond organ playing that accompanied a lone cat night-walking through the movie's celebrated title sequence by Saul Bass.

Moon River
Audrey Hepburn | 1961

A million male hearts fluttered when the angelic-looking Audrey Hepburn, as troubled young socialite Holly Golightly, sang this beautifully simple song by Henry Mancini and Johnny Mercer in *Breakfast at Tiffany's*—the most romantic of romantic comedies.

Island in the Sun
Harry Belafonte | 1957

The movie drama *Island in the Sun* proved controversial when it was released because of its interracial themes, but its theme song recorded by Harry Belafonte, one of the film's stars, was more positively received.

My Heart Will Go On
Céline Dion | 1998

One of the most over-played singles of all time, this tear-jerking theme from the mega-grossing film *Titanic* turned Canada's Céline Dion from one of the biggest female vocalists in the world into a phenomenon—and, apparently, she didn't even like the song the first time she heard it!

Knockin' on Heaven's Door
Bob Dylan | 1973

Bob Dylan wrote the highly evocative soundtrack to *Pat Garrett and Billy the Kid*, which included the outstanding and much-covered track "Knockin' on Heaven's Door." Dylan's score wonderfully echoed the majesty and mythology of the Old West explored in Sam Peckinpah's film—and Dylan also made a cameo appearance as a loner simply known as "Alias."

The Lady Is a Tramp
Frank Sinatra | 1957

The Rodgers and Hart musical *Pal Joey* made for a great movie showpiece for Frank Sinatra, Rita Hayworth, and Kim Novak. As well as Sinatra's absolute showstopper "The Lady Is a Tramp," the film also featured the wonderful songs "I Could Write a Book," "Bewitched, Bothered, and Bewildered," and "My Funny Valentine."

You Never Can Tell
Chuck Berry | 1964

John Travolta and Uma Thurman memorably cut a rug to the sound of Chuck Berry on the dance floor of sleazy club Jack Rabbit Slim's in Quentin Tarantino's cult masterpiece *Pulp Fiction* in 1994.

Little Brown Jug
Glenn Miller Orchestra | 1953

The archetypal Hollywood biopic, *The Glenn Miller Story* faded out in classic style. A tearful June Allyson, as Glenn Miller's wife, knowing that her husband had disappeared in a flight over the English Channel, listened to the Christmas morning radio as his band played "Little Brown Jug," the number he'd specially arranged for her. Weep on.

Everything I Do (I Do It for You)
Bryan Adams | 1991

It was apparently turned down by British soul star Lisa Stansfield, but Canadian rocker Bryan Adams made this theme to the film *Robin Hood: Prince of Thieves* one of the biggest international hits of the '90s. It spent seven weeks at the top of the U.S. Billboard chart and became the longest-lasting Number One in U.K. chart history—16 consecutive weeks in the top spot.

Music from the Movies

I Wanna Be Like You
Louis Prima | 1967

Jump-jive specialist Louis Prima swung with the best of them as the voice of King Louie—the orangutan who thinks he "can learn to be human too"—on this soundtrack highlight to Walt Disney's classic animated film *The Jungle Book*.

A Woman in Love
Marlon Brando and Jean Simmons | 1955

Formerly "moody" Marlon Brando surprised everyone by playing Sky Masterson, and singing no less, when the lighthearted musical take on Manhattan lowlife *Guys and Dolls* moved from the Broadway stage to the big screen. He sang this track and "I'll Know" as duets with Jean Simmons, but also sang the classic track "Luck Be a Lady" solo.

The Blues Brothers: Music from the Soundtrack
John Belushi and Dan Aykroyd | 1980

John Belushi and Dan Aykroyd as Jake and Elwood Blues—characters created for the hit TV show *Saturday Night Live*—sang the lead vocals on this cult soundtrack accompanied by an all-star guest list. Legends Ray Charles, Aretha Franklin, and James Brown, and Memphis music veterans Steve Cropper, "Duck" Dunn, and Matt Murphy all appeared in the fast-moving chase comedy *The Blues Brothers*, which managed—in some curious way—to capture the essence of '60s soul music.

Shower Theme from *Psycho*
Bernard Herrmann | 1960

Composer Bernard Herrmann wrote the music for many major films, from *Citizen Kane* in 1941 to *Taxi Driver* in 1976, with some of his most celebrated scores being composed for Alfred Hitchcock's movies. But his most musically iconic sequence by far must be the shrieking violins that accompanied the infamous shower scene in the movie *Psycho*.

Cabaret
Liza Minnelli | 1972

Visually a long way from Christopher Isherwood's stories of pre-war Berlin, *Cabaret*–the tale of goodtime girl Sally Bowles–was given an entirely new Bob Fosse-choreographed complexion by Liza Minnelli and songwriters John Kander and Fred Ebb. Liza's tremendous vibrant rendition of the title song was one of the best tracks from one of the best screen musicals since the golden days of the '50s.

Good Ol' Boys
Waylon Jennings | 1980

One of the new country "outlaw" singers of the '70s, Waylon Jennings' tough, no-nonsense brand of country rock graced scores of albums. But this track, his theme to the popular '80s TV series *The Dukes of Hazzard*–for which Jennings was also the off-screen narrator–was, by far, his most famous hit. And with the recent release of *The Dukes of Hazzard* movie, "Good Ol' Boys" looks set to find a whole new generation of fans.

THE MUSIC IS THE MESSAGE

Words and music can be very powerful tools in getting a message across, a fact not lost on preachers, politicians, and protesters throughout history. It's hardly surprising that since the advent of popular music, songwriters and musicians have regularly used it to express their particular point of view to millions of listeners. In the '60s, it even had a name—"protest music"—and it focused mainly on the civil rights movement and the war in Vietnam. There have been countless examples of banner-waving music, be it leftwing folk songs or political punk, feminist anthems or simple statements of religious faith. Whatever the cause or creed, the charity or controversy, every ideology is likely to have found a musical voice at some time or another, and many musicians have tried to make a difference with their music.

With God on Our Side
Joan Baez and Bob Dylan | 1963

Lyrics like "You don't count the dead when God's on your side" were teamed with a very emotive performance at an emotive event. Bob Dylan teamed up with politically active folk singer Joan Baez to sing his "With God on Our Side," at the 1963 Newport Folk Festival, spearheading the burgeoning "protest music" movement.

I Am Woman
Helen Reddy | 1972

Written and performed by Australian singer Helen Reddy, this became one of *the* anthems of the women's movement that was beginning to flourish in the early '70s—"I am woman, hear me roar."

Where Have All the Flowers Gone?
Pete Seeger | 1956

A catalyst in the folk song movement of the '40s, '50s and '60s, Seeger was responsible for co-writing and developing many politically conscious songs, including the well-known hits "Turn Turn Turn" and "If I Had a Hammer." "Where Have All the Flowers Gone?" is one of his most celebrated compositions.

Another Day in Paradise
Phil Collins | 1989

The former Genesis drummer started his solo career with the classy "In the Air Tonight," but he's often remembered for this socially conscious Grammy Award-winning song. In this thought-provoking track, the unlikely-looking superstar reminded us how lucky we are and asked us to consider the plight of the world's homeless.

Imagine
John Lennon | 1971

John Lennon's utopian dream of the world remains one of the most inspirational songs in popular music, though at the time of its release many questioned the multimillionaire's rejection of material wealth as he unforgettably sang, "Imagine no possessions…"

Ruby, Don't Take Your Love to Town
Kenny Rogers | 1969

Rogers' relaxed delivery on this track belied the understated anguish in a tale about a wheelchair-bound Vietnam vet unable to fulfill his marital duties. It was actually written years before by Mel Tillis in response to the Korean War. Timely, and strangely poignant.

Big Yellow Taxi
Joni Mitchell | 1970

Canadian singer-songwriter Joni Mitchell's "Big Yellow Taxi" is still one of the best musical pleas for nurturing the environment—"They paved paradise and put up a parking lot"—though nothing much has changed more than 30 years later.

Do They Know It's Christmas?
Band Aid | 1984

With worldwide sales of over seven million in its first year, this charity single recorded to aid Ethiopian famine was organized and written by Boomtown Rats' Bob Geldof and Ultravox's Midge Ure, and had a lineup that included Sting, Phil Collins, U2, Spandau Ballet, and other stars of British rock. It was the inspiration for the Live Aid concerts the following summer, and is still a seasonal favorite today.

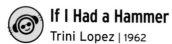

If I Had a Hammer
Trini Lopez | 1962

One of the biggest manifestations of the folk revival in commercial terms was Mexican-American singer Lopez' energetic version of this Pete Seeger song, especially when performed live to an enthusiastically participating audience—"Love between my brothers and my sisters, all over this land."

Lifestyles of the Rich and Famous
Good Charlotte | 2002

East Coast post-grunge rock at its finest, this was the track that brought Good Charlotte to a whole new generation of rebels without a cause. Taken from their album *The Young and the Hopeless*, the titles really do say it all.

My Sweet Lord
George Harrison | 1970

Despite the legal wrangling over whether he'd unintentionally copied the melody for this track from The Chiffons' "He's So Fine," this was one of George's most accessible spiritual works and a transatlantic Number One.

Rebel without a Pause
Public Enemy | 1987

Public Enemy was the original rap-as-political-protest group. Their militant stance became a template for other, often-opportunist outfits that were not as committed as them. The controversial, revolutionary lyrics and heavy beats on tracks like "Rebel without a Pause" made their *It Takes a Nation of Millions to Hold Us Back* one of the most influential hip-hop albums ever made.

Nine to Five
Dolly Parton | 1980

Humorously dedicated to the workingwoman, "Nine to Five" was the title song to the office-power comedy film starring Dolly Parton, Jane Fonda, and Lily Tomlin. One of Dolly's biggest hits, this single made it to Number One on the American Billboard chart—an early example of girl power.

I-Feel-Like-I'm-Fixin'-to-Die Rag
Country Joe and the Fish | 1967

Political protest met psychedelia in the music of Country Joe McDonald, and it did so most famously in this humorous anti-war song, which was recorded at the height of the conflict in Vietnam: "One, two, three, what are we fighting for?"

Again
Faith Evans | 2005

On this track, Notorious B.I.G's widow delivered, over a retro '70s groove, a raw and very personal account of her turbulent life—"If I had to do it all again, I wouldn't take away the rain"—and a tirade against the media, and the trappings of wealth and fame.

What's Going On
Marvin Gaye | 1971

Responding to what he saw was wrong with post-Vietnam America, Marvin Gaye radically broke out of the Motown mold when he produced and performed this ambitious concept album. He combined multi-layered dubbing and sound montages with highly emotional lyrics written from the perspective of a Vietnam vet about drugs, crime, war, poverty, ecology, you name it.

Come Away Melinda
Tim Rose | 1967

"Come Away Melinda" was a chilling after-Armageddon record from singer-songwriter Rose, written by folk-scene songwriters Fred Hellerman and Frank Minkoff. A wide range of artists, including Judy Collins, Uriah Heep, and folk pioneers The Weavers have also recorded versions of this song.

Born in the U.S.A.
Bruce Springsteen | 1984

The patriotism of the underdog was how many saw New Jersey rocker Springsteen's apparent flag-waving on this unforgettable anthem. But listening carefully to the lyrics reveals his genuine concern for his fellow countrymen, especially the Vietnam veterans who faced a lot of hardship when they returned home from the war.

Stand by Your Man
Tammy Wynette | 1968

Feminist it's certainly not. Country singer-songwriter Wynette declaring, "sometimes it's hard to be a woman" was more the response of conservative America to the women's movement, albeit from a female perspective. Then a huge hit, this is now something of a period piece.

The Revolution Will Not Be Televised
Gil Scott-Heron | 1976

American poet and musician Scott-Heron's proto-rap outpourings—with titles like "The Revolution Will Not Be Televised" and "Whitey on the Moon"—were highly political statements combined with a jazz-rock backing to make them more accessible to a wider audience. This powerful track remains his most popular.

There But for Fortune

Phil Ochs | 1966

Although inevitably coming under the shadow of Bob Dylan, Phil Ochs' brand of protest folk was certainly equally strong in its own right—no-holds-barred songs like "Ballad of the Cuban Invasion," "Draft Dodger Rag," and "Here's to the State of Mississippi" were straight to the point. This, his best-known song, was also a huge hit for Joan Baez.

Shipbuilding

Robert Wyatt | 1982

This moving piece of modern protest pop, written during the Falklands War by producer Clive Langer and Elvis Costello—who covered it the following year—was concerned with the moral dilemma of the welcome employment provided by the war machine.

Damaged Goods

Gang of Four | 1978

With the pessimistic bleakness of the late-'70s "industrial" New Wave, British students the Gang's first EP release—featuring the tracks "Damaged Goods," "Love Like Anthrax," and "Armalite Rifle"—was political punk at its best.

Earth Song

Michael Jackson | 1995

Although Jackson was criticized for arrogance and for having a "messiah complex" with the release of this song—his pompous performance at a British award ceremony was famously disrupted by Jarvis Cocker of Britpop band Pulp—the lyric was actually a powerful one. "Earth Song" made an emotional plea, that many identified with, for a world going to hell in a handbasket.

Give Peace a Chance
Lenny Kravitz and the Peace Choir | 1991

Lenny Kravitz's huge success was preceded by a number of well-received projects, including this highly original version of the John Lennon anthem, released as a comment on the Gulf War. The Peace Choir ensemble included Yoko Ono, Sean Lennon, and a host of music stars.

Talking Vietnam Potluck Blues
Tom Paxton | 1968

This super-hip satire from folk singer Paxton was about the dope-smoking servicemen in Vietnam who were trying to make the best of a bad war: "We all lit up and by and by the whole platoon was flying high..."

San Francisco (Be Sure to Wear Some Flowers in Your Hair)
Scott McKenzie | 1967

This hippie hit was written by John Phillips of The Mamas and The Papas. Along with The Beatles' classic "All You Need Is Love," it was *the* anthem of the "summer of love"—"If you come to San Francisco, summertime will be a love-in there."

I Will Survive
Gloria Gaynor | 1979

Disco diva Gaynor had a massive chart topper with this sort of feminist-oriented "My Way" that established itself as a sing-along standard on the cabaret circuit—and a gay anthem as well—that we can all join in with. Come on, everyone: "I'm not that chained up little person still in love with you..."

Every Grain of Sand
Bob Dylan | 1981

Of all the religious songs Bob Dylan wrote during his born-again period, this was certainly the most effective, and the least evangelical. The skepticism of his agnostic side was still apparent as he contemplated humility, "Sometimes I turn, there's someone there, other times it's only me." Kinda awesome.

Livin' for the City
Stevie Wonder | 1973

Stevie Wonder showed his street cred in this heartfelt plea—"If we don't change the world will soon be over"—for the urban plight of millions of black Americans.

19
Paul Hardcastle | 1985

Based on the fact that the reported average age of soldiers serving in the Vietnam conflict was just 19, Paul Hardcastle came up with this surprising, but groundbreaking, dance hit, which used repetition and rock-hard beats to get its compelling message across.

Candle in the Wind 1997
Elton John | 1997

Originally penned as a tribute to Marilyn Monroe, this track took on a new resonance when the lyrics were specially adapted and Elton John sang the new version at Princess Diana's funeral in Westminster Abbey. On release, this became the fastest-selling hit of all time in both the U.S. and the U.K., debuting at Number One and raising heaps of cash for charity.

War
Edwin Starr | 1970

One of Motown's finest vocalists, soul singer Edwin Starr made his strongest statement with this track proclaiming the absolute futility of war. Simple, straightforward, and with that great Starr voice to hammer it home, this went to Number One in the American charts and became an anthem of the anti-war movement.

I'm a Woman
Peggy Lee | 1962

From male songwriting team Leiber and Stoller, this song was Peggy Lee's pre-women's lib celebration of feminine power, albeit one safely on the married domestic front—"I can rub and scrub 'til this house shines just like a dime, feed the baby, grease the car, powder my nose at the same time."

Sign o' the Times
Prince | 1987

Hi-tech, but also highly musical in the conventional sense, Prince's dazzling style was in a more restrained mood on "Sign o' the Times," one of the most compelling anti-drugs songs on record.

Relax
Frankie Goes to Hollywood | 1983

Liverpool group Frankie Goes to Hollywood, with their out-gay front men, raised hackles with this single and its controversial music video—its message basically being relax for better sex. "Relax" went on to become one of the most successful disco-orientated records of all time and it is now a huge gay anthem.

Let's Talk about Sex
Salt-N-Pepa | 1991

Not as naughty as the title suggests, this fun, funky, and feminist number was about getting girls to be vocal about sex—while bopping about to a cool beat. With this timely track at the height of the AIDS crisis, the hip-hop duo presented a positive safe sex message and scored a hit in the process.

Proud
Heather Small | 2000

"What have you done today to make you feel proud?" asked British vocalist Heather Small, formerly of the band M People. While not really hitting on its initial release, the track became a popular motivational song and the anthem for the London 2012 Olympics bid.

We Are Family
Sister Sledge | 1979

The gay rights lobby adopted this slice of anthemic disco-soul from four-piece girl group Sister Sledge—who really were all sisters—and it still resonates today. "We Are Family" is almost guaranteed to get groups of women up onto the dance floor.

One in Ten
UB40 | 1981

Long before "Red, Red Wine" gave them their break into the U.S., UB40 distilled the feelings of powerlessness felt by many in the early '80s with this reggae-tinged tirade against British Prime Minister Margaret Thatcher. The "One in Ten" refers to U.K. unemployment levels at that time, and it certainly struck a nerve.

Ballad of the Green Berets
Staff Sergeant Barry Sadler | 1966

Among the many records that were written about the Vietnam conflict, this was one of the few blatantly patriotic songs and it was a massive U.S. hit. Co-written and performed by a genuine combatant who had served in 'Nam until he was injured by a booby trap, it now survives only as a musical museum piece.

Strange Fruit
Billie Holiday | 1939

With stark, horrific imagery depicting the lynching of African Americans—"Pastoral scene of the gallant South, the bulging eyes and the twisted mouth"—Holiday used the full force of her tortured soul to immortalize an explicit political poem by Lewis Allan. A pioneering moment in American music history.

Leaving on a Jet Plane
Peter, Paul, and Mary | 1969

Written by John Denver and performed by America's most popular folk group, Peter, Paul, and Mary, this is one of the most evocative songs of departure ever released, "Hold me like you'll never let me go."

Unpretty
TLC | 1999

The follow-up to the all-conquering hit "No Scrubs," this song was female R&B group TLC's unique take on the world's obsession with face values, with the girls saying you have to look within to find real beauty. Only T-Boz could come up with a line like: "You can buy all the make-up that MAC can make..."!

Independent Women
Destiny's Child | 2000

"Independent Women" was an "I Am Woman" for the '00s generation from the biggest female group of the decade. On this tremendous chart topper from the soundtrack to the movie *Charlie's Angels*, the girls' avowed that women are the ones with the financial clout these days—and don't it feel good to pay your own way!

Eton Rifles
The Jam | 1979

Paul Weller's Mod revivalists represented the natty-suited side of the British New Wave music scene. Their songs, like those of punk contemporaries The Clash, addressed social issues in Margaret Thatcher's Britain—this disdainful track ridiculed the wealthy and privileged students of the prestigious Eton College.

Streets of Philadelphia
Bruce Springsteen | 1993

This haunting title track was written for Jonathan Demme's Oscar-winning AIDS movie *Philadelphia* starring Tom Hanks. It sees Springsteen move away from his usual rock guitars to a powerful and sympathetic study of the effects of disease on the body and spirit, and it won him a slew of Grammys as well as an Academy Award for Best Song.

CULT COLLECTIBLES

What makes a particular artist a "cult" favorite, or a record a "collector's item?" Obscurity helps: if you can't find something without scouring the Internet or secondhand record stores, then almost by definition it's collectible—particularly if it's rated so bad that it's good! Oddity is another cool criteria: eccentric performers like Tiny Tim or Nervous Norvus, and wacky records from "Flying Saucer Rock 'n' Roll" to "Jilted John" and "Alley Oop," are all memorable, if a little mad. Then there are the wonderful one-offs, the never-to-be-repeated gems for only the most dedicated treasure-seeker—Bob Dylan in front of a symphony orchestra or the first album ever entitled "psychedelic." And, of course, there are hundreds of tracks, some hits in their time, others not, that are still sought after for nothing less than being, in their own unique way, great pieces of music.

Psychotic Reaction
The Count Five | 1966

This single is a slice of classic garage-band psychedelia, complete with angst-ridden lyrics and plenty of attitude, from a bunch of West Coast youngsters who initially wore Dracula-style capes on stage—a true one-off cult collectible.

Banana Boat (Day-O)
Stan Freberg | 1957

Freberg released this hilarious and brilliant parody of Harry Belafonte's "Caribbean" hit, which includes a great moment in which the laidback bongo-playing session musician suddenly gets squeamish at the mention of a "black tarantula"—great stuff.

Gary Gilmore's Eyes
The Adverts | 1977

Never averse to some shock tactics, archetypal Brit punks The Adverts had their biggest seller with this song based on the true story of American murderer Gary Gilmore, who volunteered for his eyes to be used for transplant operations after he was executed by a firing squad.

I Put a Spell on You
Screamin' Jay Hawkins | 1956

Skull-toting Jay Hawkins had a whole theatrical stage act based on the "occult" image created around this song, which was aped years later by the likes of Arthur Brown and Black Sabbath. Hawkins screamed his way through this weirdly unique track, which became his signature song and was included in the Rock and Roll Hall of Fame's crucial list of 500 Songs That Shaped Rock and Roll.

A Hard Rain's A-Gonna Fall

Bob Dylan | 1994

Dylan deconstructs his songs gig by gig, but in 1994 he embellished rather than altered the original—and what an embellishment! This version, recorded live at a Japanese Buddhist temple accompanied by the full Tokyo New Philharmonic Orchestra, was breathtaking.

Shaka Zulu

Ladysmith Black Mambazo | 1987

Thrust into the international spotlight after Paul Simon featured them on his *Graceland* album, South African vocal group Ladysmith Black Mambazo perfectly showcased the simple beauty of their ten-voice, close-harmony singing on the album *Shaka Zulu*, which Simon also produced.

I Know an Old Lady (Who Swallowed a Fly)

Burl Ives | 1952

A leading light in the American folk revival of the '50s, Burl Ives' best-remembered records are the ones most popular with children, including "Blue Tail Fly," "Big Rock Candy Mountain," and this delightful piece of nursery nonsense.

Have I the Right

The Honeycombs | 1964

This is memorable for being perhaps one of the worst records to hit the charts during the '60s beat boom, with its infuriating organ sound and a clumping rhythm from girl drummer Honey Lantree. In these days of postmodern irony it is, of course, now considered some sort of classic.

Fire
The Crazy World of Arthur Brown | 1968

One of the more ludicrous manifestations of the flower power era, face-painted Arthur Brown went on stage wearing a burning helmet—which occasionally caused near-infernos at his live gigs—and singing "I am the god of hell fire." Needless to say, "Fire" was his only hit.

Angie Baby
Helen Reddy | 1974

Quirky-voiced Helen Reddy didn't get any quirkier than on this Number One single, the story of an odd-ball girl who has "special" friends that come out of her radio, until one night.... Spooky!

Echo Beach
Martha and the Muffins | 1980

Ultimately one-hit wonders, the Marthas—there were two of them—and their Muffins hail from Toronto and were some of the best purveyors of the New Wave sound, the "poppier" successor to punk. We defy you to listen to Echo Beach and remain seated!

Transfusion / Dig
Nervous Norvus | 1956

As Nervous Norvus, singer Jimmy Drake performed some of the most far-out singles of the '50s—indeed of all time. His U.S. hit "Transfusion," which included lines like "My red corpsuckles are in mass confusion," was concerned with a blood transfusion after a car accident, while its flipside "Dig" was a jive-talking epic in the cool jazz vernacular of the day: "D-I-G means you know the score, so dig, dig, dig, and dig some more."

Wuthering Heights
Kate Bush | 1978

Inspired by the classic novel of the same name by Emily Brontë, this song became a huge U.K. smash—partly due to Kate Bush's histrionics during her TV appearances to plug the song—and it still sounds weirdly intriguing today.

Graduation Day
The Four Freshmen | 1956

The smooth-sounding four-part harmonies of the jazz-orientated Four Freshmen and the high school subject matter of their hit "Graduation Day" were a direct influence on The Beach Boys, who actually covered this song in '65.

C30, C60, C90 Go!
Bow Wow Wow | 1980

New Wave band Bow Wow Wow was one of several short-lived post-punk projects masterminded by the Sex Pistols' manager Malcolm McLaren. This single—dedicated to the home taping of music that was rather ambitiously predicted to bring down the record industry in the '80s—was a minor landmark in that it was initially only released on cassette.

Space Oddity
David Bowie | 1969

From its immortal opening line, "Ground Control to Major Tom..." this haunting Bowie track is unforgettable. A pun on the Stanley Kubrick movie epic *2001: A Space Odyssey*, Bowie's first hit single was doubly topical, as it was released when man was landing on the moon for the very first time.

Mystery Train
Elvis Presley | 1955

One of Elvis' earliest hits, this was derived from Junior Parker's
1953 cut "Mystery Train"–also recorded on Sun Records–which was
itself an adaptation of "It Takes a Worried Man," beloved of folkies
and skifflers everywhere.

Tiptoe through the Tulips
Tiny Tim | 1968

A real oddity, bizarre-looking Tim, aka Herbert Khaury, with his
goofy teeth, straggly hair, and silly clothes crashed into the charts
while strumming a tiny ukulele on this quickly-irritating falsetto
version of a trite song from the '30s. It takes all kinds...

Moon's Rock
Moon Mullican | 1958

As a crucial pioneer of country boogie, which had a direct impact
on rock-'n'-roll, Texan singer and pianist Moon Mullican gave us
such gems as this and influenced the likes of Jerry Lee Lewis. His
byline, "King of the Hillbilly Piano Players," says it all.

I'm Waiting for the Man
Velvet Underground | 1967

On this track, with its insistent, throbbing music, the Velvets were
proto-punk nearly a decade before anyone else. A radical rock
song–perhaps more so now, given today's largely bland standards–
in which Lou Reed takes us to uptown Manhattan to score drugs
from "The Man."

Fairytale of New York
The Pogues featuring Kirsty MacColl | 1987

This bittersweet classic folk ballad, inspired by an Irish novel by
J. P. Donleavy, was a rousing musical reference to the Irish New
York connection, though Kirsty MacColl and The Pogues' lead singer
and songwriter Shane McGowan were actually born in England.

My White Bicycle
Tomorrow | 1967

Produced by Pete Townshend of The Who, this vintage sample of
pop psychedelia from the innovative British band Tomorrow seemed
oh so trendy back then—now it's merely dated. But, as with all but
the very best pop records, 'twas ever thus.

This Wheel's on Fire
Julie Driscoll and Brian Auger's Trinity | 1968

Memorable for being used as the theme to the TV comedy series
Absolutely Fabulous several decades after it hit the charts in 1968,
this cover of a classic Bob Dylan song is still Ab Fab today.

Money (That's What I Want)
The Flying Lizards | 1979

Experimental group The Flying Lizards released this wonderful
version of an early Motown side written by Barrett Strong, but
made famous by The Beatles. With a quirky, spoken vocal by
Deborah Strickland, it's no wonder this cover has been used on
the soundtracks to so many recent movies.

Rocket 88
Jackie Brenston and His Delta Cats | 1951

In 1951, the fastest saloon on the roads in the U.S. was reckoned to be the eight-cylinder Oldsmobile 88, nicknamed the Rocket in advertisements. This record celebrating the car was written by Ike Turner, but credited to vocalist Brenston, and is sometimes considered the first real rock-'n'-roll record, though many would beg to differ.

461 Ocean Boulevard
Eric Clapton | 1974

The epitome of the relaxed style that has characterized much of Clapton's work since the '70s, this album included typically laidback versions of Johnny Otis' "Willie and the Hand Jive" and Bob Marley's "I Shot the Sheriff."

Stranded in the Jungle
The Cadets | 1956

At the novelty end of doo-wop, "Stranded in the Jungle" was a great example of the vocal-group-as-storytellers. Crazy but cool, it was The Cadets' biggest hit.

Louie Louie
The Kingsmen | 1963

"Louie Louie" was a three-chord song, primitively recorded and great to dance to—pure rock'-n'-roll. Written by Richard Berry, it became a one-hit wonder for archetypal garage band The Kingsmen. Shortly after its release, rumors began circulating that the song contained obscene lyrics, which led to an investigation by the FBI. But after many months, the investigators could only report that the record was "unintelligible at any speed we played it."

Green Onions
Booker T and the MGs | 1962

The MGs—the Memphis Group—were the house band at Stax records and they are best known for this organ-led 12-bar instrumental. Low down and funky, "Green Onions" was an understated instrumental anthem in the soul and R&B clubs of the mid '60s, and it became a cult classic from thereon.

Heartbreak Hotel
Stan Freberg | 1956

Freberg's parodies of the hit pop songs of the day were never bettered than on his out-of-control-echo version of Elvis Presley's first chart smash—"I split my jeans...that's the third pair today."

Watch Your Step
Bobby Parker | 1961

His lack of hits has rendered Parker's name something of a side note in the rock history books, but he was a dynamic performer. "Watch Your Step," his one big single, broke new ground in frantic guitar-led R&B and was often covered by British groups throughout the '60s.

Float On
Modest Mouse | 2004

Modest Mouse—an indie rock trio from deepest, darkest Issaquah, Washington—honed their distinctive musical style in a makeshift space beside vocalist Isaac Brock's mom's trailer. If that doesn't qualify this as cult music, nothing will! "Float On" is one of their most recent hits, taken from their acclaimed album, *Good News for People Who Love Bad News*.

Midnight Special
Lonnie Donegan | 1955

Like much of Donegan's early repertoire, "Midnight Special" was originally a Huddie Ledbetter song dealing with the recurring themes of prison life and the railroad. This was what the skiffle craze, crucial in the genesis of British rock, was all about.

Roadrunner
Jonathan Richman | 1975

American musician Jonathan Richman's simplistic but poetic lyrics and oddball singing style struck a chord with New Wave audiences in the mid '70s. Recorded with his group The Modern Lovers, "Roadrunner" made it into the U.K. Top Ten in 1977.

Electric Bath
Don Ellis | 1967

Don Ellis was an experimental bandleader who was interested in extending the boundaries of time signatures and tonality. He had his biggest success during the psychedelic era with the release of this acclaimed album.

Readings from *On the Road*
Jack Kerouac and Steve Allen | 1959

Although Beat Generation writer Jack Kerouac seemed oddly uncomfortable in the TV recordings of these sessions, Steve Allen's sympathetic piano accompaniment to Kerouac's readings from his seminal novel *On the Road* were typical of the poetry and jazz fusions that were so very fashionable at that time.

My Baby Just Cares for Me

Nina Simone | 1957

Hard-edged Simone—and that went for her personality as much as her voice—crafted a huge catalog of work in her career, a stunning mixture of jazz, gospel, blues, and folk standards. "My Baby Just Cares for Me" became her signature song.

Mellow Yellow

Donovan | 1967

Memorable partly because it triggered a short-lived and foolish craze among weekend hippies for smoking dried banana skins, the effervescent folk rock song "Mellow Yellow" remains one of the must-have collectibles of the flower power era.

Rock On

David Essex | 1973

Apparently a lightweight pop crooner, David Essex nevertheless wrote and recorded some highly atmospheric singles in the early '70s, not least this evocation of the spirit of rock-'n'-roll, which was his only U.S. hit.

Rockin' behind the Iron Curtain

Bobby Marchan | 1959

R&B singer Bobby Marchan is best known for the hit "There Is Something on Your Mind" but he also recorded this track—one of several examples, that are now collectors' items, of the Cold War (along with flying saucers and bug-eyed monsters) being used as the grain in the rock-'n'-roll songwriter's mill.

This Is What We Find
Ian Dury and the Blockheads | 1979

Along with the hits "Sex and Drugs and Rock and Roll," and "Hit Me with Your Rhythm Stick" this was a fine example of the British band's witty lyrics and a surreal slice of classic Dury philosophy— "A sense of humor is required, amongst the bacon rind."

Spirit in the Sky
Norman Greenbaum | 1969

The catchy fuzz-guitar riff and "spiritual" lyrics made this a one-off chart smash for singer-songwriter Norman Greenbaum. The song was also a U.K. hit for Doctor and the Medics in 1986 and for *Pop Idol* contestant Gareth Gates in 2003 for the charity Comic Relief.

Baby Let's Play House
Elvis Presley | 1955

The stuttered intro to this early Elvis track, recorded when he was with Sun Records, heralded the archetypal echo-chamber sound of early rockabilly—much imitated, often lampooned, but never equaled.

I Just Don't Understand
Ann-Margret | 1961

Swedish-American sex-bomb Ann-Margret strutted her stuff through several big budget, yet lightweight musicals in the '60s, including *Bye Bye Birdie* and Elvis' *Viva Las Vegas*, but at the start of the decade she made this sultry single, which was later covered on stage from time to time by none other than The Beatles.

Burma Shave
Tom Waits | 1977

An epic, on-the-road song about doomed companions driving across the flat American landscape on their way to nowhere. On this track, Waits' rasping, smoker's-cough voice crossed beat generation lyrics with an after-hours jazz club delivery.

Wooly Bully
Sam the Sham and the Pharaohs | 1965

The Pharaohs' chugging rhythms and nonsense lyrics made for one of the great R&B dance one-offs, which hit the Number Two spot in the U.S. and was chosen as Record of the Year by *Billboard* magazine—"Hey watch it now," Sam!

Straight Out the Jungle
The Jungle Brothers | 1988

Cool, clever, funky, and amusing—The Jungle Brothers' first rap album was a million miles away in spirit from the dubious macho menace and posturing of many others, then and since.

Back Country Suite
Mose Allison | 1957

Allison's modern jazz piano was surprisingly effective in evoking the humid, blues-drenched atmosphere of his native Mississippi. His debut album had the whole of one side dedicated to ten short vignettes, but only one of the ten, "Blues," included vocals. It was later featured on The Who's *Live at Leeds* album under the title "Young Man Blues."

Closer
Joy Division | 1980

Regarded by some as the most important rock album of the '80s, *Closer* was the chilling aftermath to lead singer Ian Curtis' suicide, including as it did powerful, gloomy, posthumously released tracks in which his unsettling, despairing voice was at its most articulate.

Message from James Dean
Bill Hayes | 1955

Not so much jumping on the bandwagon as jumping on the hearse, this single—which followed Hayes' Number One hit "The Ballad of Davy Crockett"—was an opportunistic opus released in the aftermath of the sudden death of Hollywood icon James Dean.

Happenings Ten Years Time Ago
The Yardbirds | 1966

It was curious how R&B stalwarts The Yardbirds—Eric Clapton's original group—evolved into a proto-psychedelic band. In fact, guitar giants Jeff Beck and Jimmy Page were sharing lead honors when this seemingly innovative single was made. Like I said, curious.

Jilted John
Jilted John | 1978

Jilted John—the alter ego of actor and musician Graham Fellows—was a lovelorn loser whose single was punk's most successful excursion into parody. With a whining monologue over an archetypal New Wave super-speed backing track, "Jilted John" was a weird, but very memorable, novelty hit: "Gordon is a moron..."

Psychedelic Lollipop
Blues Magoos | 1966

The first album ever to have "psychedelic" in its title, this was the second LP by the Bronx-based Magoos, whose banal attempt at early acid rock included outfits trimmed with neon lights that lit up during high points in their performances—definitely one for collectors only!

Flying Saucer Rock 'n' Roll
Billy Lee Riley and His Little Green Men | 1957

The best rockabilly record to address the UFO phenomenon was this single by Billy Lee Riley and his aptly named Little Green Men—a marvelous Sun Studio lineup that included the great Jerry Lee Lewis on piano.

Cool for Cats
Squeeze | 1979

London New Wavers Squeeze came up with some highly literate songs reflecting local life that sound as fresh today as they did the day they were written, most notably their hits "Up the Junction" and "Cool for Cats."

The Day the Circus Left Town
Eartha Kitt | 1956

Eartha Kitt's vocals had a purring, almost nasal quality that was effective on all manner of material, from suggestive come-ons like "Let's Do It" and "I Want to Be Evil" to evocative oddities like this track. Her trademark purring vocal style was also one of the reasons she was famously cast as Catwoman in the '60s TV show *Batman*.

Our School Days
The Monitors | 1957

School days became a favorite subject as soon as the teenager was first "discovered" by marketing men in the early '50s. This single by Louisiana vocal group The Monitors is now a doo-wop obscurity, but is well worth the hunt for collectors of such gems.

Treat Her Right
Roy Head | 1965

Although the high-octane "Treat Her Right" made it into the American charts, country singer Roy Head's energetic style did not easily appeal to mainstream country and western audiences, but it did assure him of a cult following.

F.E.A.R.
Ian Brown | 2001

As frontman for Manchester band The Stone Roses, Ian Brown had already earned his reputation as one of rock's most visionary talents. His solo efforts cemented this, and "F.E.A.R." was among the best examples of his penchant for stomping vocals and a compellingly lush sound.

September on Jessore Road
Allen Ginsberg | 1971

The great American poet and visionary Ginsberg wrote this epic condemnation of the West's policies towards the Third World, inspired by the sight of starving children in India. This song-poem featured Ginsberg on Indian harmonium and Bob Dylan—who said he'd wept when he read the poem the night before the recording session—on piano, organ, and guitars. Awe inspiring.

Cars

Gary Numan | 1979

Numan's monotone voice and deliberately sterile synth sounds gave his most famous hit, from the album *The Pleasure Principle*, a two-dimensional feel in keeping with its gloomy ambitions. The success of "Cars" has often overshadowed the rest of his career, but Numan remains influential today and still has a dedicated cult following.

Alley Oop

The Hollywood Argyles | 1960

A studio-created group made up of session musicians, one-hit wonders The Hollywood Argyles had a hip-talking American Number One with "Alley Oop"—a novelty song based on a popular caveman comic strip character.

The Animal Song

King Perry | c1954

Songwriters and producers seemed fond of sound-effects records in the early days of rock-'n'-roll and in this rare example of early studio trickery we take a visit to the zoo for some bestial bop.

Candy Man / The Devil's Got My Woman

The Rising Sons | 1966

Before either of them were well known, blues-rock luminaries Ry Cooder and Taj Mahal made their recording debuts as part of this Californian band. The Rising Sons recorded a total of 22 tracks between '65 and '66, but only released this single before disbanding the same year. Their album was finally brought out in 1992—the stuff of legends.

The Weight
The Band | 1968

This classic rock hit was written by the influential Canadian-American group's main songwriter and guitarist Robbie Robertson. This crucial fable from The Band's debt album pointed out the one direction in which "new country"—before the phrase was ever thought of—would be moving.

This Town Ain't Big Enough for the Both of Us
Sparks | 1974

The oddball duo of brothers Russell and Ron Mael, who came out of the Los Angeles club scene, specialized in quirky songs with an almost camp edge to them; and this was the big one.

Poisoning Pigeons in the Park
Tom Lehrer | 1957

When so-called "sick" humor was fashionable in the late '50s in response to the work of stand-up comics like Mort Sahl and Lenny Bruce, the time was just right for college professor Lehrer's irreverent take on life. His most popular songs included "The Old Dope Peddler," "The Masochism Tango," and this concert favorite.

Some Other Guy
The Big Three | 1963

This was one of the best singles to come out of that "second division" of groups from Liverpool, England during the Merseybeat boom. Despite being signed with Brian Epstein, the manager of The Beatles, The Big Three never quite managed to fulfill their potential or make it in a big way outside of their hometown.

The Holy Modal Rounders, Vol. 1

The Holy Modal Rounders | 1964

The Rounders were an anarchic Greenwich Village duo, whose often chaotic mix of bluegrass, blues, and pre-rock pop was delivered in a "progressive old-time" style that defied classification. Gigs and recording sessions were often a hit-and-miss affair, yet their debut album and its follow-up the next year were highly influential on the emerging "underground" rock scene of the mid '60s.

(Every Time I Hear) That Mellow Saxophone

Roy Montrell | 1956

New Orleans session guitarist Roy Montrell co-wrote this song for Specialty Records. A frantic jump-band rocker of a record celebrating the virtues of that most mellow of instruments, the saxophone—"Every time I hear that mellow saxophone I wanna rip it, rock it, really bop it..."

Love Will Bring Us Back Together

Roy Ayers | 1979

Known as one of the prophets of jazz, Roy Ayers first showed a precocious talent for music while he was still knee-high to a saxophone, and he pioneered the now ubiquitous hip-hop sound back in the early '70s. Most of his solo albums have been out of print for a long time, but plenty of his jazz-funk classics, including this single, are now available for download.

FURTHER READING

- **Absolute Beginner's Guide to iPod and iTunes, 2nd Edition**
Brad Miser, Que Publishing, 2005

- **The Art of Downloading Music**
Steve Levine, Sanctuary Publishing, 2004

- **Caution! Music and Video Downloading: Your Guide to Legal, Safe, and Trouble-free Downloads**
Russell Shaw and Dave Mercer, Wiley Publishing, 2004

- **Complete Idiot's Guide to MP3: Music on the Internet**
Rod Underhill and Nat Gertle, Alpha Communications, 2000

- **The Future of Music: Manifesto for the Digital Music Revolution**
Dave Kusek and Gerd Leonhard, Berklee Press, 2005

- **How to Do Everything with MP3 and Digital Music**
Dave Johnson and Rick Broida, McGraw-Hill Osborne Media, 2001

- **How to Do Everything with Your iPod and iPod Mini, 2nd Edition**
Guy Hart-Davis, McGraw-Hill Osborne Media, 2004

- **iPod and iTunes for Dummies, 2nd Edition**
Tony Bove and Cheryl Rhodes, For Dummies, 2004

- **iPod and iTunes: The Missing Manual, 3rd Edition**
J. D. Biersdorfer, Pogue Press, 2005

- **MP3 and the Infinite Digital Jukebox: A Step-by-step Guide to Accessing and Downloading CD-Quality Music from the Internet**
Chris Gilbey, Seven Stories Press, 2000

- **Music Online for Dummies**
David Kushner, For Dummies, 2000

- **The Rough Guide to iPods, iTunes and Music Online, 2nd Edition**
Peter Buckley and Duncan Clark, Rough Guides, 2005

ABOUT THE AUTHOR

With a background as a musician on the '60s rock scene, **Mike Evans** has been a music fan all his life. He began writing on popular culture in the '70s, and, has also worked as a broadcaster on local radio. As a freelance writer, he has written many music articles and books, and his work has appeared in a variety of newspapers and magazines, including *Sounds*, *Elle*, *The Guardian*, and *Melody Maker*.

Since the late '80s, Mike has been working in book publishing, commissioning and editing over 80 titles on music, movies, and fashion. As an author, he has also been very successful. His books include the much acclaimed *The Art of the Beatles* and the best-selling *Elvis: A Celebration*, which he researched and wrote in collaboration with the Presley Estate in Memphis. He is also the author of *NYC Rock*, *Waking Up in New York City*, *The Marilyn Handbook*, published by MQ Publications, and, most recently, the major biography *Ray Charles: The Birth of Soul*.

Mike is as busy as ever with his writing, and still finds time to play the saxophone, in a non-professional capacity. Mike lives and works in London, dividing his time between writing, his freelance editorial consultancy, and his wife, children, and grandchildren.

artist index

song & album index